The Foreign Policy Centre

www.fpc.org.uk

The Foreign Policy Centre is an independent think-tank launched by Prime Minister Tony Blair (Patron) and former Foreign Secretary Robin Cook (President) to examine the impact of globalisation on foreign and domestic policy. The Centre has developed a distinctive research agenda that explores the strategic solutions needed to tackle issues which cut across borders – focusing on the legitimacy as well as the effectiveness of policy.

The Foreign Policy Centre has produced a range of **publications** by key thinkers on subjects relating to the role of non-state actors in policymaking, the future of Europe, international security and identity. These include: *The Post-Modern State and the World Order* by Robert Cooper, *Network Europe* and *Going Public* by Mark Leonard, *NGOs Rights and Responsibilities* by Michael Edwards, *After Multiculturalism* by Yasmin Alibhai-Brown, *Trading Identities* by Wally Olins and *Third Generation Corporate Citizenship* by Simon Zadek.

The Centre runs a rich and varied **events programme** at The Mezzanine in Elizabeth House – a forum where representatives from NGOs, think-tanks, companies and government can interact with speakers who include prime ministers, Nobel Prize laureates, global corporate leaders, activists, media executives and cultural entrepreneurs from around the world.

The Centre's quarterly magazine, *Global Thinking*, is a regular outlet for new thinking on foreign policy issues. Features include profiles, exclusive interviews with decision makers, and opinion pieces by the Centre's permanent staff and associated authors. The Centre runs a unique internship programme – the UK's only route for new graduates into the foreign policy arena.

About the authors

Mark Leonard is Director of The Foreign Policy Centre. He has written widely on European Integration and legitimacy including his acclaimed pamphlet *Network Europe* (Foreign Policy Centre 1999) and *The Pro-European Reader* (with Dick Leonard, Palgrave 2002). His work on "Rebranding Britain" led to an international debate on branding countries and inspired the Foreign Secretary to launch Panel 2000, a taskforce to advise him on promoting Britain abroad. Mark has built on this with influential studies on public diplomacy including the report *Going Public: Diplomacy for the Information Society* (with Vidhya Alakeson, Foreign Policy Centre 2000). Mark writes and broadcasts extensively on British, European and International Politics. He has acted as a consultant on identity for foreign governments and private companies. Mark previously worked as senior researcher at the think-tank Demos and as a trainee journalist at *The Economist*.

Catherine Stead , the project director for the public diplomacy research, was seconded to The Foreign Policy Centre from the British Council. Prior to that she spent three years working for the British Council in the Baltic States. She has ten years experience of conducting public diplomacy in the field.

Conrad Smewing joined the Foreign Policy Centre as Mark Leonard's assistant after completing an MPhil in International Relations at the University of Cambridge.

Public Diplomacy

Mark Leonard
with Catherine Stead and Conrad Smewing

The Foreign Policy Centre

First published in 2002 by
The Foreign Policy Centre
The Mezzanine
Elizabeth House
39 York Road
London
SE1 7NQ

Email info@fpc.org.uk
www.fpc.org.uk

Cover by David Carroll

Typesetting by Rory Fisher

Public Diplomacy

Acknowledgements

This report is the conclusion of a two-year research project, and is the product of many people's ideas, hard work and experience. We gratefully acknowledge both the financial support and intellectual engagement of the following organisations, who made this research project possible: The British Council, The Royal Norwegian Ministry of Foreign Affairs, BBC World Service, the Design Council, and the Embassy of the United States of America in London.

This report builds on the interim report, *Going Public*, which I co-wrote with Vidhya Alakeson. The research process has only been made possible through the generosity of the British Council who first seconded Liz Noble and then Catherine Stead to the Foreign Policy Centre to direct the research and fieldwork on this project. Liz laid the foundations for the field work, while Catherine travelled to the four corners of the earth gathering data and ideas with considerable élan. Two other people have played a nodal role in managing this process: Conrad Smewing tirelessly drafted sections and gathered source material, while Laura Demetris conducted vital research, identified key contacts in the relevant countries, co-ordinated with different partners and masterminded the international travel plans. Adam Higazi also helped gather material for the appendices.

We would like to thank all those whose contributions of time, practical support, information and ideas made this report possible. Our project steering group, chaired by the ever-encouraging Sir Michael Butler, included figures with much experience of public diplomacy: HE Tarald Brautaset, Andrew Fotheringham, Jonathan Griffin, Fritz Groothues, Fred

Martenson, Dame Pauline Neville Jones and Patrick Spaven. They provided direction and helped shape the final form of this report. Edmund Marsden who was the original inspiration for the project also provided very helpful feed-back on this report. The staff of the Foreign Policy Centre have all come together to make this possible – particular thanks must go to my assistant Phoebe Griffith for her ideas on the structure of the report and Veena Vasista, my deputy, for steering the Centre so effectively while I was engrossed in various drafts.

All those who helped to make the case study visits happen, in particular Edmund Marsden, British Council India, John Tod, British Council France, Richard Morgan, British Embassy Paris, Xavier North, French Ministry of Foreign Affairs, Robert Sykes, British Council Gulf States, Tim Gore, British Council Dubai, HE Ann Grant and Nick Sheppard, British High Commission South Africa, Robert Peirce, British Embassy Washington, Teresa Evans, British Consulate-General Boston, Sara Everett, British Information Services New York, Jeremy Eyres and Iwona Kochel, British Council Poland, Johan Meyer and Oyvind Stokke, Royal Norwegian Ministry of Foreign Affairs.

It is impossible to list all the people that we interviewed or who took part in focus groups and discussions, but in Appendix IV, we list some of the main people who were interviewed.

Mark Leonard, The Foreign Policy Centre, London June 2002

1. Introduction: Why Public Diplomacy?

Public Diplomacy: Definitions

"Public diplomacy differs from traditional diplomacy in that it involves interaction not only with governments but primarily with non-governmental individuals and organisations. Furthermore public diplomacy activities often present many differing views represented by private American individuals and organizations in addition to official government views"
(Edward Murrow, 1963, speaking as director of USIA)

"Public Diplomacy seeks to promote the national interest of the United States through understanding, informing and influencing foreign audiences."
Planning group for integration of USIA into the Dept. of State, June 20, 1997)

"I conceive of public diplomacy as being the public face of traditional diplomacy. Traditional diplomacy seeks to advance the interests of the United States through private exchanges with foreign governments. It works very much in coordination with and in parallel to the traditional diplomatic effort."
(Christopher Ross, at Brookings/Harvard Forum, January 16, 2002)

"The purpose of public diplomacy is to influence opinion in target countries to make it easier for the British Government, British companies or other British organisations to achieve their aims. The overall image of Britain in the country concerned is of great importance – but this is not to say that it is the only factor. The most important factor will usually be the actual policies of the British Government and the terms in which they are announced and explained by Ministers. In most countries a broadly internationalist posture will be positive. A narrow and open pursuit of national interests at the expense of others will be negative. For example, the Government's handling of the beef crisis in the summer of 1996 had a negative effect not only on Britain's ability to get its way on other EU issues, but also on the view taken of Britain in many non-EU countries."
(Sir Michael Butler, former British permanent representative to the European Union, 2002)

It took the tragedy of September 11th for the 'battle for hearts and minds' to rise once again to the top of the international political agenda. After the fall of the Berlin Wall, the United States had lost its urge to spread its values and messages to the four corners of the world, and gradually run down many of the propaganda and information tools which it had relied on so heavily during the cold war – emasculating the USIA and paring the Voice of America and Radio Free Europe down to almost residual proportions.

In developing countries and former communist states, no real attempts were made to build a popular consensus for liberal democracy, and reformist governments were expected to persuade their citizens to swallow the bitter pill of structural adjustment without much sugar-coating. Today policy-makers are still trying to come to terms with the depth of hostility to America and the West. Of course it is not just a problem of communication. Poverty, exclusion from the world economy, double-standards on trade and democracy (particularly the West's support for discredited and repressive regimes), the predatory behaviour of some western multinationals and a range of policy positions on issues from the Arab-Israeli conflict to the sanctions against Iraq all fuel tensions. But it is equally clear that communication and building relationships do have a part to play if we are going to avoid slipping into a battle between the West and the rest. There is a double challenge: showing that what you represent is more attractive than the alternative, and keeping your coalition together – which is no longer as easy as it once was during the Cold War.

Ironically, it is the end of the Cold War which has made public diplomacy more important: the spread of democracy, the media explosion and the rise of global NGOs and protest movements have changed the nature of power and put ever greater constraints on the freedom of action of national governments. This means that – even more than during the Cold War – we need to invest as much in communicating with foreign publics as with the governments that represent them if we are to achieve our objectives.

There are many examples of issues where the attitude of overseas publics plays a determining role in the government's ability to pursue its foreign policy objectives. The Afghan and Kosovo conflicts saw powerful military coalitions risk defeat, not in the field, but in the media battleground for public opinion. In Rwanda ethnic conflict was mobilized through inflammatory radio broadcasts rather than military command chains. The global anti-capitalist demonstrations have illustrated a new diplomatic environment where state and non-state actors compete for the public's attention. During the British BSE crisis the French government, in breach of EU law, banned British beef largely in response to public fears about its safety. In a global economy, countries compete against each other for investment, trade, tourists, entrepreneurs and highly skilled workers.

In each of these cases perceptions of Britain and other countries combine to create an enabling or disabling backdrop for each situation. It is clear that propaganda will not persuade populations in reluctant countries to support the war against terror – but perceptions of Western motivations as imperial or self-interested can damage chances of success, and divergent national debates can cause tensions which could eventually break up the international coalition. Independent or national sources of news will not block out calls to arms from tribal radio stations, but they can act as a counterweight by presenting a calm overview of the ongoing tensions and giving access to information which may be of critical importance (Rwanda had only 14,000 phones but some 500,000 radios). Promotional campaigns for British beef have a limited impact on the fears of consumers, but work to show the quality of British science and the integrity of our vets did play a role in assuaging the French public's suspicion. And many studies have shown that campaigns to change the perceptions of countries like Ireland, Spain or New Zealand can create a premium for products and services as well as playing a role in attracting investment and tourists.

The American academic Joseph Nye has argued that the power of attraction can be an important complement to more traditional forms of power based on economic or military clout. He draws a distinction between 'hard' and 'soft' power: "Soft power works by convincing others to follow, or getting them to agree to, norms and institutions that produce the desired behaviour. Soft power can rest on the appeal of one's ideas or the ability to set the agenda in ways that shape the preferences of others". Because most of the messages that people pick up about a country are beyond the control of national governments - books, CDs, films, television programmes, brands or consumer products with national associations, events, etc. - the activities of governments and other organisations are going to have an impact at the margins, seeking to clear paths and give impetus to the most positive messages for mass audiences while working directly on niche audiences.

This report explores how countries could work to correct the negative perceptions produced by the marketplace and harness the power of other actors to increase their own voice on the world stage. It is based on a two-year research programme that explored how some of the largest industrialised countries (Britain, France, Germany, and the United States) conduct public diplomacy. It also looked at the public diplomacy of Norway, a country that has used public diplomacy to good effect. The research included of interviews with senior policy-makers in a number of organisations representing those countries abroad. It explores how public diplomacy works in practice in six case study countries (India, South Africa, United States, France, Poland, the United Arab Emirates) where we have conducted our own qualitative research through focus groups and interviews with young professionals, as well as drawing on quantitative research carried out by MORI for the British Council. We have supplemented this with interviews with experts in academia and the communications industries.

In the chapters that follow we draw a number of important conclusions. First we argue that there is not a sufficient commitment of resources to this new type of diplomacy. All governments pay lip-service to the way that the rise of global communications, the spread of democracy, the growth of global NGOs and the development of powerful multilateral organisations have changed the nature of power within societies, and altered the craft of government and diplomacy. But these changes have not been adequately reflected in the way that governments as a whole deploy their resources, or the way that foreign services in particular organise themselves and relate to the institutions they fund.

Joseph Nye makes this point very strongly, "If you look at expenditures in the American budget, we spend about 17 times as much on military hard power as we do on all our foreign representation, the State Department budget, foreign aid as well as the Voice of America and all the exchange programs lumped together. There is something wrong with that picture". The picture in the UK is very similar, with the Ministry of Defence receiving 18 times the amount of the FCO (£24.2 billion compared to £1.3 billion). The investment in public diplomacy is dwarfed by the returns that come from successful work – and the cost of failure. For example, the 200,000 foreign students that the British Council works to attract every year earn £5 billion for British higher education. Equally, the disastrous images that came out of Foot and Mouth have already cost an estimated £2 billion in lost tourist revenue.

But it goes beyond the relationship between spending on reactive military power and preventative diplomacy. Diplomatic institutions need to move beyond the old model of bolting on a few new units and recruiting a couple of extra staff from NGOs – changes which are essentially cosmetic. Instead, what is needed is a fundamental re-balancing of the diplomatic offer and a larger investment in it. Foreign services must transform themselves from being reporters and lobbyists on reactive issues to shapers of public debates around the world. There are a number of key lessons that we draw:

- Governments do not pay enough attention to the way that stories will be received abroad. The main way to engage with mass audiences in other countries is not through embassies on the ground, but by working through foreign correspondents in your own capital.

- Western governments are competing with each other in 200 countries when they have bilateral interests in just a fraction of that number. This unhelpful competition undermines objectives in developing countries while preventing a proper focus of resources on those countries where they have a bilateral interest.

- Governments need to change the tone of public diplomacy - so that it is less about winning arguments and more about engagement. In an environment where citizens are sceptical of government and sensitive about post-colonial interference, public diplomacy institutions need to be much more interactive - building long-term relationships and understanding target groups rather than delivering one-way messages.

- Conspicuous Government involvement in public diplomacy can be counter-productive. Governments are not great persuaders. By working through parties that people will trust – from NGOs and Diasporas to brands and political parties – they are more likely to build trust and achieve their objectives than by acting as spokespeople themselves.

- Foreign services and public diplomacy institutions need to build the possibility of crises into their planning by developing greater budgetary flexibility. and public diplomacy SWAT teams that can be mobilised at very short notice.

- All countries need to prove their relevance - rather than take it for granted. For example, survey data shows that even where people have positive feelings about Britain, the fact that they see it as a country in decline means that they will turn to others about whom they feel less favourable.

- Public diplomacy should be focused on the countries which are most relevant to our interests - not those which are easiest to influence.

We argue for a new type of multilateral public diplomacy – retooling embassies to become lobbying and policy-exchange organisations; creating an infrastructure to link up political parties and NGOs across borders to create a common policy space; and planning proactive communication campaigns.

2. The Three Dimensions of Public Diplomacy

The phrase 'public diplomacy' is often used as a euphemism for propaganda. Journalists have portrayed it as a crude mechanism for delivering messages that may or may not reflect the facts. Naomi Klein's vituperative piece for *The Guardian* is not untypical: "It's no coincidence that the political leaders most preoccupied with branding were also allergic to democracy and diversity. Historically, this has been the ugly flipside of politicians striving for consistency of brand: centralised information, state-controlled media, re-education camps, purging of dissidents and much worse."

In fact public diplomacy is about building relationships: understanding the needs of other countries, cultures and peoples; communicating our points of view; correcting misperceptions; looking for areas where we can find common cause. The difference between public and traditional diplomacy is that public diplomacy involves a much broader group of

Image 1: The Circle of Public Diplomacy

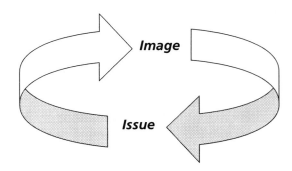

Image

Issue

people on both sides, and a broader set of interests that go beyond those of the government of the day.

Public diplomacy is based on the premise that the image and reputation of a country are public goods which can create either an enabling or a disabling environment for individual transactions. Work on particular issues will feed off the general image of the country and reflect back on to it – in both positive and negative directions. For example, Britain's reputation for tradition will help heritage brands such as Asprey's sell their products, and their advertising campaigns will also reinforce Britain's reputation as a heritage nation. Equally Norway's reputation for work in international mediation will help persuade the different factions in Sri Lanka that they are an honest broker, which will in turn add to their reputation for peace.

There is a hierarchy of impacts that public diplomacy can achieve:

- Increasing people's familiarity with one's country (making them think about it, updating their images, turning around unfavourable opinions)

- Increasing people's appreciation of one's country (creating positive perceptions, getting others to see issues of global importance from the same perspective)

- Engaging people with one's country (strengthening ties – from education reform to scientific co-operation; encouraging people to see us as an attractive destination for tourism, study, distance learning; getting them to buy our products; getting to understand and subscribe to our values)

- Influencing people (getting companies to invest, publics to back our positions or politicians to turn to us as a favoured partner)

In order to achieve these goals, governments need to be clear that public diplomacy cannot be a one-dimensional process of delivering messages.

One way of conceptualising public diplomacy is as a grid of three rows and three columns.

Table 1: The Three Dimensions of Public Diplomacy

Purpose	Reactive (hours and days)	Proactive (weeks and months)	Relationship building (years)
Political/Military			
Economic			
Societal/Cultural			

On one axis are the spheres on which it is played out: **political/military**, **economic** and **societal/cultural**. These will carry different weight at different times, and in different contexts. For example in a developed country like Singapore economic messages will be important; in Pakistan political messages will matter more; in Zimbabwe messages about British diversity will act as a counterweight to allegations of racist imperialism; while in European Union countries like France and Germany all three spheres will be important. Events like September 11th can obviously change the priority of different issues and put the political/military sphere at the top of the agenda in all countries.

In each of those spheres, we can characterize three dimensions of public diplomacy activities:

- Reacting to news events as they occur in a way that tallies with our strategic goals

- Proactively creating a news agenda through activities and events which are designed to reinforce core messages and influence perceptions

- Building long-term relationships with populations overseas to win recognition of our values and assets and to learn from theirs

Each of these dimensions operates according to a different time-scale. Reactive news takes place in hours and days, proactive communications and perception changing activity is planned in weeks and months, while building relationships can take years before it generates a return. The dimensions also demand different skills and organisational cultures. News management needs to be flexible, reactive and plugged into the government machine. Proactive communications demands highly developed communications skills, strategic planning and the budgets, resources and the expertise to organize events that can capture the imagination. Building relationships depends on earning high levels of trust, creating a neutral and safe environment, and can often best be done at one remove from government.

Each country has a different set of institutions to manage its public diplomacy strategy. Some are part of government, others are independent. Each will have its own mission and priorities, but in order to practice public diplomacy effectively, it is important to examine the institutions as a spectrum and see whether there are gaps between the institutions which are not yet filled. In chapter seven, we examine the UK institutions in this way and set out some lessons for how the spectrum can be improved, but first let us examine the three dimensions.

News Management

The first dimension is the management of communications on day-to-day issues, reflecting the growing need to align communications with traditional diplomacy.

The need to ally communications with traditional diplomacy is described by the US diplomat, Christopher Ross, who was brought back from retirement to mastermind public diplomacy with the Muslim world: "I conceive of public diplomacy as being the public face of traditional diplomacy. Traditional diplomacy seeks to advance the interests of the United States through private exchanges with foreign governments. Public diplomacy seeks to support traditional diplomacy by addressing non-governmental audiences, in addition to governmental audiences, both mass and elite. It works very much in co-ordination with and in parallel to the traditional diplomatic effort." This implies that embassies must plan public diplomacy strategies for all of the main issues they deal with – and explore the communications angles of all their activities.

This job is complicated by that fact that it is increasingly difficult to isolate different news stories for different audiences, foreign and domestic. Although most TV, radio and print media are still created with a national or local audience in mind, their networks of foreign correspondents will ensure that messages do get transferred from one region to another. As Secretary of State Colin Powell put it: "During Desert Storm we really were seeing this 24-7 phenomenon, at least in my judgment, for the first time … I used to tell all of the members of my staff, 'Remember, when we are out there on television, communicating instantaneously around the world, we're talking to five audiences.' One, the reporters who ask the question – important audience. Second audience, the American people who are watching. The third audience, 170 capitals who may have an interest in what the subject is. Fourth, you are talking to your enemy. It was a unique situation to know that your enemy was getting the clearest indication of your intentions by watching you on television at the same time you were giving that message. And fifth, you were talking to the troops. Their lives were on the line."

Paradoxically, so called 'domestic stories' like the race riots in Oldham and Burnley, or the outbreak of Foot and Mouth in Britain, or the success of Le Pen in the French elections are often as important as 'foreign policy' stories in making an impact on others. Alastair Campbell, the Director of Communications in 10 Downing Street, described this vividly in an interview with the authors: "in relation to Foot and Mouth there was this collision between domestic and foreign audiences. Part of our message, once we'd focused on it as a crisis management issue being led from the top, was that the Prime Minister was involved, sleeves rolled up, talking to the farmers regularly.... I admit that this didn't cross my mind, you get these dramatic pictures of the Prime Minister wearing yellow suits and walking around a farmyard, and in America they think 'Christ! He's got to wear a yellow suit! And he's the Prime Minister.' Because that's all they're seeing. Our media will only ever give a narrow context, go further abroad it gets even narrower. And so, that is the kind of thing you've got to really think carefully about".

As well as unforeseen crises, there are predictable domestic events which come up every year and can play out badly in other countries. Examples include the release of the British Crime Survey which frequently results in erroneous stories such as, "Crime in London is worse than New York", or the start of the Norwegian whaling season which results in acres of negative press coverage around the world (for Norwegian public diplomacy strategy, on whaling and other issues, see Appendix

II). The domestic departments involved in these issues need to provide the foreign service with the notice and the information they need to contextualise the stories.

Strategic Communications

Governments have traditionally been good at communicating their stances on particular issues, but less effective at managing perceptions of the country as a whole. One of the reasons for this is the fact that different institutions have been responsible for dealing with politics, trade, tourism, investment and cultural relations. But on many issues, it is the totality of messages which people get about the UK which will determine how they relate to us. This is the second dimension of public diplomacy: the strategic messages we promote about the UK.

Sir Michael Butler, who was previously the British Permanent Representative to the EU, argues that perceptions of the country generally will shape the diplomatic environment: "We need to have a broad image which is favourably perceived in the key countries where we are based. If your government is perceived as self-interested, reactionary and unhelpful, it will seriously hamper your ability to get your way – as the US is finding at the moment." And unless there is a lot of work done over a long period of time to create a more positive context, all attempts at communications will be viewed with added suspicion. An official in the White House confessed to me, "We haven't made any attempts to communicate with ordinary Arabs unless we are bombing them or imposing sanctions on them – I wouldn't like us if I were them."

In the economic realm, the power of national perceptions is even clearer. As products, investment environments and tourist destinations become more alike, it is becoming difficult to differentiate oneself in terms of quality alone. Tapping into a deeper sense of identity can help companies differentiate themselves from their competition. Opinion surveys show that three quarters of Fortune 500 companies actually see 'national identity', or place of origin, as one of the key factors that influence their decisions about buying goods and services. Many consumer companies have built on this insight. In the 1990s, the German AEG (Algemeine Elektrische Gesellschaft) ran a publicity campaign in Britain which was based around redefining their initials as 'Advanced Engineering from Germany'. The centrepiece of their advertising campaign was that it was a 'German' company, a national image that represented brand quality.

Strategic communication is different from relationship-building. It is a set of activities more like a political campaign: setting a number of strategic messages, and planning a series of activities over a year or so to reinforce them. This is what Charlotte Beers describes as magnification: "An impressive example was delivered by the team in ECA when they arranged to send stunning photographs of Ground Zero by Joel Meyerowitz to open in 20 countries….What I appreciate so much about this program is that it gives us an audience beyond the government officials and elites - the young and people in smaller towns as the exhibit travels to cities around these countries and reaches others through very good press coverage. That's what we mean by magnifying the results from a single event."

It is important for all the public diplomacy organisations to have a stake in the totality of messages which are put out about the country, and a sense of how they can co-operate on promoting them.

Chris Powell, the chairman of advertising company BMP DDB Needham argues that these messages must be simple: "Have very few, preferably one, message. People are exposed to thousands of messages every day. They probably recall only a tiny fraction of these. The task is to cut through this fog by imagination and repetition. A contrast between diplomacy and advertising is that in advertising an enormous amount of work goes into the preparation – boiling ideas down into very, very simple concepts, and then repeating that message over and over again until we are all thoroughly bored with it. When you are so bored with it that you feel like giving up, the listener may just have begun to register the message. So stick at it. The Drink Drive campaign has been going for years and is as relevant today as it has ever been because the message is simple, clear and logical."

But to what extent is it possible to have a single message that unites all the different players – from the British Tourist Authority to the Foreign Office? And how relevant will it be to different audiences, from citizens in the Middle East to potential investors in Australia?

Many countries have shown the power of having a clear national narrative which can unite the different stakeholders. The most famous example is probably Spain, where Miro's Espana image signaled a determination to shed the ghost of Franco and become a modern, European democracy. There are two key dangers in not creating a clear narrative. One is the idea of discordant messages. In the case of Britain, it would appear strange if the British Council heavily promoted the UK as a modern, multi-ethnic and creative island, while the British Tourist Authority simply re-iterated national stereotypes about tradition, ceremony and history. One solution to this conundrum that has been proposed is to make a virtue of the paradox and develop an identity around the idea of dynamic tradition – playing on a binary identity which was famously described by life-style guru Peter York as "punk and pageantry". It is however important to remember that there are 'givens' in how we are seen abroad. If the 'dynamic tradition' positioning is adopted, the survey data shows that our promotional efforts will need to be weighted towards the dynamic end of the spectrum as that is the area which people are most sceptical about.

There is a danger in this idea of articulated positioning. When Robin Cook established the Panel 2000 taskforce to advise him on the projection of Britain overseas, it debated long and hard which messages should be promoted before deciding on a list of five messages (reliability and integrity, creativity and innovation, Britain's heritage, free speech and fair play and openness to the world) which roughly corresponded to the interests of the five main public diplomacy institutions and allowed the different partners to carry on performing as they had done before. I have written elsewhere about the fact that perceptions of Britain are out of date and have set out a strategy to attempt to turn them round in Britain™ – the report which launched an international furore about 'Rebranding Britain'. But there are also pitfalls for any country surrounding national branding.

Many people have attacked the idea that something as complex as a national identity can be 'sold' in the same way as soap powder. This is obviously true, and clumsy attempts to market countries – even in specific sectors such as tourism – run the risk of reducing the excitement and diversity of a national culture to a homogenous, antiseptic commodity. The clearest example of this is the attempt to sell beach holidays: one image of a white beach and some blue sea is practically indistinguishable from another. When this happens, the net effect of branding is not to add value but to detract from it as the key differentiator in this sort of commodified market will be price.

People have also pointed out that the only way to fully manage a national brand is to have a totalitarian state, as most of the impressions that people get of a country come from things outside government control – such as meeting British people, buying British products and services, watching films, reading newspapers etc. Because the 'carriers of the brand' are so diverse, any attempt to sell a country that does not reflect the reality of that country is doomed to be undermined by people's actual experience. This reflects the fact that the most successful perception-changing campaigns have been carried through by countries that had undergone dramatic and genuine change – for example Spain after Franco or Ireland in the 1990s – and rooted in a commonly owned national story.

Relationship Building

The third dimension of public diplomacy is the most long-term: developing lasting relationships with key individuals through scholarships, exchanges, training, seminars, conferences, building real and virtual networks, and giving people access to media channels. This differs from the usual diplomatic practice of nurturing contacts as it is about developing relationships between peers – politicians, special advisers, business people, cultural entrepreneurs or academics. This can take place across the three spheres of public diplomacy and is aimed at creating a common analysis of issues and giving people a clearer idea of the motivations and factors effecting their actions so that by the time they come to discussing individual issues a lot of the background work has been done already. It is important not just to develop relationships but to ensure that the experiences which people take away are positive and that there is follow-up afterwards. Building relationships is very different from selling messages because it involves a genuine exchange and means that people are given a 'warts and all' picture of the country.

Research by the British Tourist Authority showed that people who come to the UK invariably report that they leave the country with a more positive impression of it than when they arrived. Joseph Nye makes this point eloquently: "It is not that the student goes back converted but they go back with a much more sophisticated idea of our strengths and weaknesses. You complexify their thinking. So they will go back and be critical of American policy on Israel or they will go back and be critical of American policy on capital punishment. But they will have a deeper understanding of why it is that Americans treat gun control differently than Europeans. This may grow out of the fact that I spent two years as a student in Britain right out of college. It took me about a month to realise, 'My God, these people are strange!' At the end of two years I thought I can see Britain's faults and I can see Britain's greatness and they are all mixed up together. I think it was in Britain's interests that I would develop a nuanced view of Britain rather than either an Anglophilic idealisation or an Anglophobic characterisation. And I think that aspect of soft power is probably most effective."

Charlotte Beers, the Undersecretary of State for Public Diplomacy in the United States, points to the staggering success of the Fulbright scheme which has been taken up by over 200 current or former heads of state: "Coming from the private sector, it's hard to find anything comparable to the sheer productivity of our Fulbright and International Visitor exchanges. The $237 million we will spend in 2002, for some 25,000 exchanges, is magnified by the 80,000 volunteers in the U.S. and matching support from many countries like Germany and Japan. Considering that some 50 percent of the leaders of the International Coalition were once exchange visitors, this has got to be the best buy in the government."

Relationship building has traditionally been seen as a process that must be conducted face to face and on a personal level. The most effective instruments for building enduring relationships are scholarships, visits and other exchange programmes that require complex planning and administration and come with a high unit cost. But as societies become more open and pluralistic, particularly in large transitional economies where the target audiences number several millions, this traditional mode of working is unlikely to reach the critical mass of people necessary to significantly affect the opinions and choices of those audiences.

To what extent will the new information and communication technologies enable the relationship building process to be scaled up to include much larger groups of people? In India, the British Council has identified a successor generation target audience of 7 million people aged between 20 and 35, nearly 90% of whom live in 25 cities, whose profile suggests that at different stages of their education and early working lives they would be receptive to the Council's information and educational services. At present the Council operates in 11 cities and at any one time provides services to about 120,000 members and visitors to their libraries and information centres.

The Council is now planning to use new approaches to online and distance learning and a specially developed online library to extend its services to a much larger clientele. The quality of the engagement with this larger audience will not be of the same order as that achieved through more traditional and expensive face to face programmes – which will continue to play an important role in India. However, by increasing to at least 300,000 over a three year period, the number of people in regular contact with the Council either face to face or online, the Council believes that it will achieve the critical mass necessary to affect attitudes and choices among the wider target groups in key cities.

The Japan Exchange and Teaching (JET) Programme

The Japan Exchange and Teaching (JET) Programme invites young college and university graduates from overseas to participate in international exchange and foreign language education throughout Japan. The programme has earned a high reputation, both in Japan and overseas, for its efforts in human and cultural exchanges, and has become one of the largest cultural exchange programmes in Japan. The program offers college and university graduates the opportunity to serve in local government organizations as well as public and private junior and senior high schools. Begun in 1987 with the co-operation of the governments of the participating countries, the programme has grown up year by year. The number of JET participants who are currently working in Japan has reached over 6,000 and the number of ex-JET participants from approximately 40 countries totals around 30,000. The JET Programme also includes a great deal of follow-up and network building. For example, the JET Alumni Association is intended to strengthen the "bonds of friendship" developed by former participants. With over 44 local Chapters in 11 countries, it currently enjoys a membership of over 10,000 individuals.

3. Competitive and Co-operative Public Diplomacy

There are some parts of the world where Western countries have a clear and incontrovertible national interest in carrying out bilateral public diplomacy work. In these countries – the world's largest economies and markets, regional powers like Nigeria or South Africa, countries of emerging strategic importance – they compete with others for access to markets, for investment, for political influence, for tourism, for immigration talent, and for a host of other things which will bring direct benefit to them alone. This is often a **competitive** zero-sum game. In these countries, there will always be a need for multilateral activities on particular issues (for example EU work on promoting multilateralism in the United States, or work in Pakistan on maintaining the coalition against terror) but because of the strong bilateral interests it will be important for many public diplomacy activities to be explicitly associated with Britain, or whichever country is promoting itself.

But these are not the only places where countries like the UK have an interest in doing public diplomacy work. In the rest of the world, there is a clear interest in carrying out work that promotes stability, economic development, human rights and good government. However, that interest differs from a bilateral interest in one key respect: it is not a uniquely British interest but is rather an indivisible interest of all Western countries. There is little purpose, for instance, in the UK competing for inward investment from Malawi, and little more in competing with the

French or the Americans to be its most influential ally. These are countries where public diplomacy should be **co-operative**.

In this chapter, we argue that it is important for public diplomacy strategies to reflect this situation, and to make a clear distinction between 'competitive' and 'co-operative' public diplomacy. The natural interest of any institution is to compete for power and influence wherever it can, and to expand the scope of its activities as much as resources allow. But we argue in this report that it makes sense to choose the countries for competition according to clear criteria, and to prioritise resources accordingly. Some people will argue that it is difficult to have a black and white picture of where our interests lie, and that attempts to prioritise are often confounded by history (who would have put Afghanistan, Sierra Leone, or Rwanda in their priority list?). But we are explicitly not arguing for a withdrawal from developing countries – on the contrary we call for a consolidation of resources into a co-ordinated multilateral programme and an end to damaging competition. It is true that there will always be shades of grey – and a need for a regular review of countries' priorities – but that cannot act as an argument against trying to create a framework for defining priorities.

Co-operative public diplomacy
In most parts of the world there is no advantage in making civil society-building activity, promoting good governance or promotion of Western values, an activity explicitly originating from Britain. It is not just that it could be better and more efficiently carried out multilaterally; there are important disadvantages in conducting this activity under an umbrella of national self-promotion.

In the first place, by divorcing activity designed to promote democracy, human rights and the rule of law from a country-specific context, you also divorce it to an extent from a neo-colonial context that is damaging to its effectiveness. Bilateral British attempts to promote democratic reform in Zimbabwe, or French attempts to do the same in its own former colonies like Algeria, unavoidably run into the rhetorically powerful response that colonial control is being re-exerted through the back door of human rights universalism. Removing the national branding from this work retains all of its usefulness to the West, and increases its effectiveness by side-stepping the sensitivities that understandably surround it.

A second, and equally damaging, aspect of attempting to carry out this kind of vital Western public diplomacy bilaterally is that it can lead to 'great game'-style competition for influence which detracts from the good such work could be doing. The French or the British essentially attempt to create 'zones of influence' in the developing world – zones that centre naturally on the former colonial empires, and which seem justified because of an emphasis on the importance of historical links for country prioritisation in the calculations of, for instance, the British Council. This agenda of competition is an institutional hangover from colonial days (or in the case of the United States a result partly of self-proclaimed exceptional status) and is, objectively speaking, absurd. Despite increased co-operation on substantive issues (for example, the co-operation on Africa initiated by Robin Cook and Hubert Vedrine) there is still a good deal of competition on public diplomacy. Part of this is simply to do with institutional rivalry between the BBC World Service and RFI or between different posts – some of it has also to do with the fact that the BBC's impact has in the past been measured by its global audience figure rather than its reach among target audiences.

Table 2: Competitive and Co-operative Public Diplomacy

	Countries Targeted	Interest	Mode of operation
Competitive (roughly 50 countries)	G20	Political influence	Bilateral (on issues specific to us)
	EU 15 + Accession	Military co-operation	
	Top 20 Tourist, Trade and Investment Partners	Trade	Multilateral (on issues we share with others)
		Investment	
	P5	Tourism	
	NATO	Coalitions in IGOs	
	Diaspora Links	Policy exchange	
Co-operative (roughly 140 countries)	All other developing countries	Promoting democracy, good governance, human rights, regional stability	Multilateral

Some examples of this damaging competition in public diplomacy come from Western involvement in Afghanistan. The International Crisis Group's Asia Program Director Robert Templer claims that the rebuilding of Afghanistan has exhibited "a conspicuous failure of public diplomacy." It is vital for the success of the Loya Jirga process that it have the support of the people, a vital prerequisite of which is effective dissemination of information about the process itself. Yet, Templer argues, the UN has no independent radio system in place in Afghanistan (placing it a step behind, for instance, the Iranians and the BBC World Service) and has been slow to publish information on how the Loya Jirga will be conducted or what its aims will be. Templer argues that many Western nations have concentrated on slapping country branding on their (much-needed) aid and assistance in a competitive fashion that has the dangerous side effect of robbing the fledgling central Afghan administration of profile, legitimacy and, ultimately, stability. The French, for example, have proudly reopened the Lycee in Kabul and played on old links to Ahmed Shah Massoud in an attempt to promote their influence in the area. They also undermined the unifying symbolism of the return of the old King, Zahir Shah, by very publicly receiving the Defence Minister who had chosen to snub the King by being in Paris at the time of his return. This kind of political jockeying is highly damaging to the broad Western interest in Afghanistan and in failed states generally.

The Voice of America, the BBC World Service, Deutsche Welle and RFI compete for audience, for frequency, and for influence in the developing world when this brings miniscule additional benefits to the nations concerned (the US, UK, France or Germany). The VOA – bolstered by a large vote of funds from Congress in the wake of September 11th – has been bidding for presence on FM frequencies in Somalia against the World Service, and is in danger of causing price inflation through the large amounts they are paying for FM frequencies in the Arab World. While it is clear that that the BBC World Service has very different editorial values from VOA, and that it would damage its reputation for editorial independence if it were to join forces with it on production, it is important to ensure that competition between the two services is always worthwhile – and that it does not simply result in precious resources being squandered in a bidding war for frequencies. These concerns about editorial values do not, however, apply to other European services. It seems perverse for the BBC to be in competition with RFI in Francophone Africa, rather than joining forces and creating a European service which could serve the local populations equally well and produce modest savings for France and Britain.

Consequently, instead of running competitive public diplomacy programmes in the large majority of countries that do not have significant bilateral relations with the individual Western governments, the West should combine its resources and co-ordinate efforts on this kind of activity. If the activities of the World Service, and of the British Council in many places, amount to at the least a Western public good, then they should be harnessed as a mechanism that encourages contribution from all the governments of the West.

This would be easiest to organize – at least initially – within the European Union. Tony Blair could use the Danish EU summit this Autumn to suggest that the European Union develops a plan for co-operatively funded and executed public diplomacy activity in the vital majority of the world's countries where the members of the European Union have no *differentiated* interests, but instead a pressing *communal* need.

In the mean-time it would be sensible to create a more informal system of burden-sharing within the Western governments, where the British contribution would be the existing World Service and British Council 'good governance' activities in developing countries, and where other countries would agree to contribute complementary activity in kind or cash funding.

Britain should take a lead by deliberately down-grading the 'Britishness' of its activities in those countries and consulting allies at country level. This would bring the World Service, and also much British Council activity, into a culture that emphasises the importance of programmes for the host country, rather than the donor. This would go some way, at least, toward divorcing public diplomacy activity in the developing world from a 'great game' model of interests, which it is the accepted duty of the FCO to manage and pursue.

Competitive Public Diplomacy
A very important corollary of removing the British flag from public diplomacy activity in the majority of countries is that it affords an opportunity for truly effective prioritisation of resources in the remaining 50 or so bilaterally targeted countries. Norway is one country that has explicitly recognised this. Instead of attempting to garner influence with publics in every country where it happens to have an embassy, the Norwegian government has concentrated all its public diplomacy activity on what it regards as its six key country audiences: the US, the

UK, Germany, Russia, Japan and France (see Appendix II). The UK has more global aspirations than Norway, and so would seek to spread its influence more widely than a Spartan six countries, but the central idea of clear prioritisation for bilateral public diplomacy is a good one.

Prioritisation is a thorny issue, and one made harder by the Foreign Office's reluctance to admit to any country that it is not, in fact, central to the UK's foreign policy in one way or another.

In some areas the UK's priorities are clearer than others. Economic relations, under the remit of Trade Partners UK and Invest UK, are reasonably easy to quantify and hence prioritise. It is uncontentious that the UK should actively promote its products and businesses bilaterally amongst the largest markets, and the largest economies, in the world – at the same time including some of the most promising emerging markets. The members of the G20 and the EU, for instance, would make a good central core of countries to concentrate upon. Equally, in terms of European political influence, the UK has a clear interest in developing political links and political influence with some of the most important EU accession countries. The Britain Abroad Task Force, for instance, has recently added the Czech Republic and Hungary to its original target list of 18 countries (which already included Poland and Turkey). Important regional powers like Nigeria, South Africa and Indonesia would also be central candidates for targeted bilateral relations for any country whose interests were projected on a global stage.

This kind of prioritisation is, of course, already carried out by UK public diplomacy institutions, but the criteria used are often not sufficiently clear-eyed for the purpose. One example is the British Council's determination of country importance based on historical, as well as political and economic, grounds. This idea of rating a country's importance as a target for British public diplomacy work based in part of the extent of its historical links with the UK is code, in most cases, for its colonial links and can lead to decisions being made on the basis of our interests in the nineteenth century rather than today's pressing needs.

But the most damaging criteria applied to prioritising countries, and one that is a central part of, for instance, the British Council and the World Service's calculations regarding future activities, is that of "potential impact". Potential impact is judged on the basis of "demand for services among target groups" and "competing influences". But these seemingly innocuous criteria are in danger of putting the cart before the horse and acting as a justification for the status quo. There is a danger that decisions are taken not to prioritise key markets because the traditional public diplomacy tools (English-language tuition, educational reform, radio) are unlikely to work, rather than defining the priority countries according to objective criteria and devising strategies for making an impact in these conditions.

The division of the spectrum of public diplomacy activities into different institutions can have negative results in these situations, because each institution calculates its priorities in terms of what it thinks it can achieve through its own bundle of activities, rather than tailoring activities to the countries where it is vital that public diplomacy impact be achieved. One clear example of this concern with the ability to make an impact is the telling lack of public diplomacy work by the British Council in the USA, the richest and the most powerful country on Earth. The British Council carries out very little activity in the United States, on the basis that there is little impact that it could have on a mature democracy with a thriving domestic media and close informal transatlantic links – and because the Embassy has historically had a major information programme. But it is clear that there is an important need for public diplomacy activity in the United States, and as the case study demonstrates (see ppendix I) it is not difficult to imagine a series of activities designed around long-term relationship building, and political education which could have a considerable impact.

What is needed is a clear strategy for these different types of countries with different goals for each of the institutions. We set this out in Chapters Seven and Eight.

4. Keeping Your Head in a Crisis
Ensuring crisis responses do not divert governments from long-term goals

Public diplomacy operates in centuries, or in seconds: combining the long-term background through which events are perceived with the instant shock that can be pivotal to an international relationship. This temporal duality comes out strongest in a major crisis.

Relations with the Muslim world were framed by differing degrees of engagement from the time of the crusades, through colonial times, the creation of Israel to the Gulf War, but in an instant the attack on the World Trade Centre reframed the power dynamic in the relationship. Britain's image around the world had been defined for decades through images of the pomp, circumstance and cool reserve of the British Monarchy, but the public's reaction to Princess Diana's death in an instant buried many associations of Britain with the 'stiff upper lip'. Equally, a single night of violence at the Heysel stadium supplanted the idea of the English gentlemen in the consciousness of many European populations with its polar opposite: the hooligan.

Each shock or crisis represents an opportunity to effect radical paradigm shifts in public diplomacy, opportunities that can be seized and turned to the advantage of a country. However, the very nature of the shock makes it difficult to deal with: it is unexpected, it is out of control, it may be highly positive or highly negative in its initial effect, it can suck up enormous resources in its wake, and it is rarely repeated in the same form. Governments are not very good at planning their resources around the idea of shocks which makes it even more difficult to respond – in spite of the fact that there has barely been a year this decade which has not had a major public diplomacy shock. 2001 was perhaps atypical, but for the UK it was a year defined by its public diplomacy crises: the outbreak of Foot and Mouth disease, the collapse of the railway system, riots in Bradford, Burnley and Oldham as well as September 11th. The response to each crisis needs to be targeted, well resourced and run like a political campaign rather than a diplomatic effort. The key challenges are:

- Rapid reaction: an integrated response that will span changes in policies, the deployment of resources and communications

- Internal co-ordination

- International co-ordination

- The ability to keep track of long-term goals

Rapid Reaction and surge capability

The boxes on the next few pages summarise some of the responses in Britain and the United States to the crisis on September 11th. It was inevitable that the United States' response would be of far greater magnitude than the UK's – both because the attack took place in America, and because of the relative size and power of the American nation. But although the initial public response of the British Government was masterful – both on a symbolic and practical level – there remain a number of bureaucratic and administrative barriers that can hamper a rapid response.

The first constraint is the lack of budgetary flexibility. Because the Foreign Office's budget has been pared down over the years in the interests of cost-effectiveness, most of its resources are tied up in buildings and staff which makes it difficult to free up programme money in a crisis. This makes it impossible to develop new programmes on the scale of the American response (which was able immediately to draw on emergency funds), but also hampers the rapid deployment of staff. For example, several interviewees complained about the fact that it took weeks to get telephones and emails set up in the Coalition Information Centre in London (in contrast with the Washington office). The World Service and the British Council have more flexibility as they are more able to redeploy resources within the year or country budgets – but both will have to wait for the next financial cycle to be able to carry out strategic plans for the future. Given the frequency of 'unforeseen' shocks, it is certainly worth investigating the strategic flexibility that would be provided by a centrally-managed pot of 'crisis' money.

Another issue is geographical/physical flexibility. Ideally, institutions need a presence that can be scaled up and down without generating the adverse media attention that the closing a physical presence generates. This is something that the MOD or DFID are naturally good at. There is a case for thinking about creating a rapid-reaction public diplomacy squad that could set up in any crisis situation within 24 hours. As the Permanent Under Secretary to the Foreign Office Sir Michael Jay says: "How do you cope with surges? Much of the FCO's life is coping with surges. But MOD and DFID know how to set up in a crisis. We need a rapid reaction diplomacy that will allow us to set up a mission in Kabul in hours."

One solution might be to develop a residual capacity that can be deployed in the event of a crisis. The United States are currently reconstituting the remains of the Washington CIC as a regional team for Middle East media whose primary function would be to engage in regional dialogue. This would involve a readiness

The UK Public Diplomacy Reaction to September 11th

In the immediate aftermath of the September events, No 10 took over direct control of news management, working closely with the FCO to create an incident room to manage the day to day control of the crisis. In due course, the Coalition Information Centres (CIC) and the Islamic Media Unit were created to coordinate messages and provide a direct information response in Arabic. The Public Diplomacy Department of the FCO produced a publication, *Never Again*, which echoed an American web site with a similar purpose, and its Broadcasting and Allied Media Unit started producing regular news updates through its radio and British Satellite News networks. In addition, it embarked on a programme of targeted news articles and press briefings.

The timetable of responses was as follows:

• Within hours, BBC World Service started a 45 hour news programme - their longest ever.

• Within weeks No 10 and the FCO had established Coalition Information Centres (CICs) in Washington, London and Islamabad in cooperation with major coalition allies. They had also set up the Islamic Media Unit.

• In just over one month, UKwithNY, a previously planned major event opened in New York having been re-branded to suit the revised message.

• Within three months, the British Council had identified £2m savings and developed initial ideas for Connecting Futures (then Open Minds), a programme of action specifically aimed at connecting the Muslim and Christian worlds.

• Within three months the BBC World Service increased its hours of output in Urdu, Arabic, Pashto, Persian and Uzbek by between 18 per cent and 104 per cent.

• Over the next three months, the British Council continued to operate in Pakistan and processed 20,000 exam candidates and 5,000 Chevening scholarship applications as usual. In contrast, the USIS in Islamabad closed and handed over its theatre to CIC.

• Within four months the British Tourist Authority launched UKOK as a way of re-assuring people about tourism to the UK.

The US Public Diplomacy Reaction to September 11th

• From September 12th, every key government speech and policy statement was produced in six languages on the day of publication and in up to 30 languages by a few days later.

• Large numbers of interviews with US Officials took place on the Arab media.

• The State Department co-ordinated with the White House and Department of Defense to create special media centres to cover a rolling news cycle and gain a rapid-response capability.

• 'Leaflet bombs' dropped on Afghanistan, each with 100,000 flyers depicting, e.g. Taliban beating a group of women and bearing the message, "Is this the future you want for your children and women" in Pashtun and Dari.

• Single channel wind-up radios dropped on Afghanistan. VOA broadcasts in Pashtun and Dari. C-130E radio jamming planes flying over Afghanistan.

• Media tours to the U.S. for foreign journalists, particularly Muslim journalists, were mounted swiftly.

• Voice of America's Arabic service rebranded to 'Radio Sawa' ('Radio Together') broadcasting 24 hours a day and aimed at a youth market with popular music interspersed with news bulletins. Radio Sawa has a budget of c. $30m.

• Produced a four-colour booklet, *Network of Terrorism*, released on November 6th by the Bureau of International Information Programs (IIP), to visually and emotively illustrate the impact of September 11th. This product became the most widely distributed public diplomacy document ever produced. It is now in 36 different languages. Disseminated as an insert in publications like Italy's *Panorama* and Kuwait's *al-Watan* and as a full insert in the Arabic edition of *Newsweek*.

• Photographic exhibition of Ground Zero by Joel Meyerowitz to open in 20 countries. By the first-year anniversary date of 9/11, this exhibit will have opened in 60 cities. To increase relevance and broaden interest it was tailored to local circumstance, e.g. the exhibit in London, which showed pictures of the Blitz in World War II alongside.

Future US September 11th related Public Diplomacy Expenditure and Plans

• Planned US public diplomacy expenditure for FY 2003 is $595,711,000, which represents a 5.4 per cent increase over the FY 2002 funding level. Of this amount $247,063,000 is for Educational and Cultural Exchanges and $287,693,000 is for public diplomacy activities within the Diplomatic and Consular Programs.

Some planned uses of this money include:

• $15 million will be used to fund an aggressive campaign of message placement. Short video programs will air profiling the lives of certain Muslim Americans - teachers, basketball players, firemen - on targeted media outlets in nine predominately Muslim countries. The intended message is that the U.S. is an open society, tolerant and accepting of all religions, and specifically a country where Muslims are free to practice Islam.

• $17.5 million will be employed for initiatives such as American Corners, where multi-media rooms would be installed in partnering institutions in target countries to bring an American environment and experience to key audiences, especially younger generations.

• Another plan is to reinvigorate English Teaching to foreigners in their own schools, which is seen as an effective way of exposing them to American values and preparing them for productive lives in a modern world.

• The US plans to acquire television, film, and radio rights for use in Muslim-majority states to broadcast the output of existing programmes in the private sector, including current events productions, documentaries, docu-dramas and dramatic features.

• An ECA exchange program for Muslim youth, teachers and young political leaders, adapting pre-existing models and programmes to the Islamic world.

• New projects designed to educate the foreign public on the war against terrorism and the U.S. commitment to peace and prosperity across all nations
including $5.3 million for expansion of outreach programs to improve

communications and provide support for a global public diplomacy campaign.

• Enhanced International Information Program (IIP) activities, including improved content and presentation on the website via the latest technology for delivery of material to target users, who will include perceived critical international leaders and opinion makers.

• Increased translations of InfoUSA, a combined Internet and CD-ROM information product with text materials detailing U.S. laws, governance, education, society, and culture. It is updated daily on the Internet, and 30,000 CD-ROMs are distributed every six months to users worldwide. Recipients range from executive branches and government ministries to academic institutions, NGOs and media outlets.

• Increased polling by the Bureau of Intelligence and Research in Muslim countries.

• Expanded Office of Broadcast Services' coverage of special international events, remote productions, facilitative assistance efforts, dialogues and Foreign Press Centre journalist tours. These activities include working with foreign broadcasters to produce documentary reports that highlight aspects of American life, culture or community. The documentaries are then shown on national foreign television. Foreign journalist tours focus on reporting tours for journalists in strategically important regions - the Middle East, the Balkans, and South Asia - that have few or no US-based correspondents

• Some of the supplemental public diplomacy funding for 2002 will be used to magnify the benefits of Fulbright and International Visitor (IV) exchanges by, for instance, setting up an alumni data bank. 50 per cent of International Coalition leaders had once been exchange visitors to the US. The programme funds 25,000 exchanges and visits with £237 million.

• Plans for a VOA satellite news broadcast to the Middle East to compete with Al-Jazeera et al, to broadcast 24 hours a day, with funding of approximately $250 million.

to relocate and reorganise on a regular basis, liasing with some of the 35 US agencies that currently maintain an overseas presence. Alastair Campbell argues that we should adopt a similar approach in the UK: "obviously you will never ever have totally fool-proof crisis management systems, because what makes it a crisis is the fact that it's different. But, what we're going to do is have a CIC operation ready to be activated at any point that we or the Foreign Office think that it should be. With ready to roll links into other governments departments, and hopefully ready to roll links into other countries that might need to be involved....What it means in practical terms is that within every main government department likely to be involved in a crisis management situation there is a named individual, whose job is to be that person, who may at the drop of a hat be called off doing whatever they're doing at the Cabinet Office or at the Home Office and be brought into a structure with people they know and systems they know."

Internal coordination

A crisis creates an immediate split between internal and external audiences who interpret a single government pronouncement in radically differing ways. One of the great strengths of the Foreign Office is its extraordinary network of offices around the world that are able to disseminate messages – but these are often disconnected from the key messages which need to be disseminated from London.

In Britain Foot and Mouth disease, the collapse of the railways and the riots were treated as domestic issues for weeks after they broke out. The establishment of COBRA undoubtedly showed an ability to deal with surges on the domestic side but this was not related to an international strategy. Several of the foreign correspondents we interviewed complained about the lack of access and information as the crisis unravelled. And although the DCMS were consulted as the impact on tourism became clear, the fact that the Government tends to involve departments rather than non-departmental public bodies meant that the British Tourist authority was not involved in COBRA. Foot and Mouth took on such monumental proportions that it was eventually treated as an international issue – unlike the problems with the railways and the race riots which have been treated exclusively as domestic stories. The structural problems around news management are discussed in greater detail in chapter seven.

Alastair Campbell explains the importance of centralising communications in a crisis: "The thing about crises is that you never know where they're going to come from. Foot & Mouth: we didn't know that was going to happen. When it does happen the risk is you default to an assumption that your existing structures will be able to cope. Now the point about crises is that they don't always cope. What may make it a crisis is that your existing structures aren't able to manage. You do have to throw things out, and get on with absolutely relentless focus. Whatever the enquiries are going to say on foot and mouth, the truth is that in many ways we did actually perform miracles by getting it under control as quickly as we did. A lot of that was through, admittedly in my view too slow, centralisation: things being brought to the centre. All the different bits of government likely to be involved being locked in together. When you talk about a huge international story, like September 11th, that gets ever more difficult. You've got to work out, where are the main points of activity and information? Obviously America and Afghanistan were the main two. You had Pakistan, you had the whole Middle East situation as a factor. And then you had other zones of opinion."

The importance of getting clear leadership from the top of government is confirmed by Tucker Eskew, Bush's appointee to the Coalition Information Centre in London: "In the history of the US global communications efforts co-operation has been, at times, lacking. Generally it is intermittent and in fact our efforts have been least successful and most prone to innervations and attack from various media, or governmental quarters, when it was seen as uncoordinated and of little interest to the chief executive of our government, namely the President. Conversely, the history of our efforts shows success and lack of such attacks when the President is viewed as interested ... co-operation and executive interest and integration really are crucial going forwards, based on history and recent experience."

International Co-ordination

With a foreign policy crisis, the challenge for governments is often not simply to manage their own messages to foreign and domestic audiences but to try and co-ordinate the messages of different coalition partners. In many ways the Kosovo conflict was a wake-up call on this which inspired governments to try to create an effective strategy for dealing with communications.

Alastair Campbell explains how important it is to ensure a consistent voice between capitals and institutions: "Dealing with this required a degree of co-ordination between capitals which was not there in the early days. The real problem with the 'convoy incident', for example, was not just that it happened – for people accept that there will be accidents in war – but that different things were said in different parts of the operation, as we speculated and thought aloud before the facts were known. The resulting confusion was damaging."

The Coalition Information Centre was developed to ensure that communications in Afghanistan were handled effectively. With offices in London, Washington and Islamabad, it was designed to follow the clock and ensure that the difference in time-zones would not allow the Taleban to dominate news agendas while coalition press offices were still ensconced in their beds. The Washington office was essentially a bilateral US-UK operation, but the office in London had representatives from across the coalition including countries like Russia and Norway. The routine was extremely effective, with daily conference calls chaired by Karen Hughes in the White House and Alastair Campbell in Downing Street, an intranet with lines to take on the issues of the day, a research team with a brief to develop strategic messages and plan events which could carry them, and an electronic grid of future activities so that the timing of announcements and stories could be planned strategically.

Long and short-term vision

The most difficult challenge is managing the relationship between short-term crisis management and long-term relationship building. In the heat of the moment, there is a danger of undermining both the institutions and the messages that governments are trying to promote for the long term.

With an event as dramatic as September 11th there is enormous pressure on institutions to drop long-term plans and concentrate on the crisis to the exclusion of all else. There is a danger that structures which have been built up over years are completely superseded. The new structures such as the Coalition Information Centre are built up out of nowhere with a different chain of command, usually going down from the White House or Downing Street rather than through the FCO or the State Department. We have seen above why it is important to have a tightly managed, targeted, well resourced team dealing with communications. But once the initial structure has been set up it is important to build links with the organisations and people who will be working in these areas long after the crisis has elapsed – if not there is a danger of that knowledge disappearing as it did after Kosovo. This is often the opposite of what takes place, for example in Islamabad the USIA was closed down when the Islamabad Coalition Information Centre was formed.

Different institutions need to operate according to different time-frames. Those which focus on fostering long-term relationships need to develop strategies over a number of years. The reason why the World Service was able to respond to the crisis in Afghanistan more effectively than any of its rivals was that it had been broadcasting in Pashtun for over twenty years and in Persian for sixty and had established a bed-rock of trust and goodwill (built upon its editorial independence) which could be drawn on in the crisis. It has also been present in Arabic since 1938 and has built up a reputation for quality journalism, which has much to do with its continued effectiveness in the current Middle Eastern crisis environment. It attracts 10 million weekly listeners in the Middle East including 16 per cent reach in Saudi Arabia; 18 per cent in Jordan; 12 per cent in Syria; and has a strong web offer in BBCarabic.com, giving 8 million monthly page impressions.

The British Council has been operating in Muslim and Arab countries for decades and built up a series of relationships which are important. In some of these countries, simply maintaining the existing levels of engagement at a time of uncertainty (as the Council did in Pakistan where it delivered 20,000 exams in October) sends out a positive message. There is a strong case for making extra resources available to public diplomacy institutions to deal with a crisis, and the institutions themselves need to become more adept at spotting the potential of a crisis as an opportunity to change the long-term relationship. But the key is to develop activities which draw on their strengths – and are in line with their long-term values.

One of the lessons of this is the importance of creating

institutions that are – to a degree – insulated from short-term political needs. If not, long-term processes will be made subservient to short-term political goals. Changing perceptions of Britain or winning support for our values in many parts of the world is not something that can be achieved in any one year or any one administration, so we must have the capacity for long term thinking and planning. That is unfortunately unlikely to be something that is possible in the Foreign Office with its shorter time-horizons.

Ambassador Anthony Quainton, former director of the US Foreign Service, explains how USIA has become less effective at delivering on its long-term goals as it has been brought closer to the concerns of the State Department: "USIA wanted to be seen as being responsive to the political agenda of the day. And that made it easier to snap up because its target was the short term foreign policy agenda of the US administration. Then it makes sense to integrate it into the State Department because that is where the day to day interaction between America and the world comes together. But it meant almost a complete erosion of the cultural mission. Exchanges or various kinds of artist's programs which used to be very much at the centre of USIA's programs in the '50s, '60s and the '70s became secondary to them in the drive to make Public Diplomacy integrated into the process of Foreign affairs and traditional diplomacy. "

One of the problems of not having a clear public diplomacy strategy is that there are no strategic messages to return to in a moment of crisis. Though they were not set in part of a formal strategy, it is possible to identify some key themes about Britain which the Government has sought to promote since 1997. The key political messages before September 11th were: "Britain is a force for good in the world" and "Britain is a leading member of the EU". The economic messages were about innovation and creativity. And the key social messages were about diversity and multiculturalism.

Each has been undermined – not through any deliberate act, nor even as a result of any specific lapses but as the cumulative impact of the governments various responses to the crisis of September 11th. In spite of the fact that the Prime Minister has been careful to bring these key messages together in his major speeches – such as the speech to the Labour Party Conference in October 2001 and his speeches in Africa, India and the US – our research shows that the collective impact of the actions has led to perceptions of Britain as "an American stooge", "a half-hearted European country", "not letting go of empire". One young educated participant in a focus group in India said: "The UK is a lackey to the US and also unclear about its role in Europe". (For further discussion of the impact of the UK's post September 11th positioning on bilateral relationships, see Appendix I, especially the France and India case studies.)

To an extent this is inevitable, but it is important to be conscious of the dangers throughout the process. Sir Michael Butler, the former British permanent representative to the European Union, argues that we need to be forever vigilant: "The Prime Minister and Foreign Secretary need to think of the consequences of the reactions of other countries when we are dealing with the United States. It is probably an illusion to think that we can add that much to our influence in the US by being more compliant than others – there are diminishing returns – but we can damage our relationship with other countries. The more we talk about 'being a bridge' or the 'special relationship' with the United States, the more we are likely to irritate other EU member states as they all think that they themselves have a special relationship with Europe – as well as underscoring our history as a reluctant European. In deciding the line to take on any issue, you need to take into account not only domestic public opinion, but the way things will be seen in Europe, America, and the rest of the world. What is said in one country is picked up in the media of other countries and vice-versa. When there is a crisis, the PM inevitably gets involved and the messages become the possession of a small group of people. It is not a deliberate thing, but one of the unintended consequences of this is that messages can go out which play badly in some parts of the world".

5. Moving Beyond Propaganda

Many of the initiatives which have been developed in the wake of September 11th seem to have fallen into what can best be described as a 'conveyor-belt' model for the transmission of information. If one reads recent debates and discussions about public diplomacy – particularly in the United States, but in other countries as well – there is a sense that many policy makers feel that the main problem is a lack of information, as if to say: "if only other people had access to the same degree of information that we have, and the same degree of insight, then they would agree with us".

The problem goes beyond crude 'psyops' activities such as dropping 'leaflet bombs' (showing a member of the Taliban beating a group of women and bearing the message: "is this the future you want for your children and your women" in Pashtu and Dari) or dropping single channel wind-up radios tuned to the VOA. The tone and feel of many initiatives is declamatory and about telling rather than proving through actions, symbols and words – or engaging in dialogue with a real intent to listen.

If we are to move beyond propaganda, the first challenge is to **understand the target audience** and start from where they are. Many organisations struggle to internalise and prepare for potential threats that do not tie in with their underlying strategic assumptions. But it is difficult to carry out successful diplomacy if you do not have ears for things that you don't want to hear. Too many Foreign Office publications and speeches are aimed at winning arguments and proving that we are right – rather than persuading audiences to change their minds. Both the FCO and the State Department produced leaflets on the attack on the

World Trade Centre which fell into this trap. Although they contained dramatic and shocking pictures which worked on an emotional level, the text was very forensic and argumentative – with sections structured around 6 bullet points explaining why the September 11th attacks were definitely carried out by Bin Laden. The problem is that these sorts of messages put out by diplomats will become enmeshed in what has been called a battleground of "your information vs. my information".

As the former advertising executives Adam Lury and Simon Gibson put it: "the answer is not more information, but a different form of engagement". That is what led the US Undersecretary of State for Public Diplomacy, Charlotte Beers, to advise American public affairs officers: "Our Goal is NOT what you say, but the response that you desire". In other words public diplomacy is not simply delivering a message to an audience – it is about getting a result. And to get a result, you need to take account of the fact that the listener's views and experience matter as much as the message that the speaker is sending.

This means being ready to explore the legitimacy of some of our most basic beliefs, from human rights and gender right down to health and safety, and environmental safeguards in different societies. It means conducting research about why people feel the way they do. A good example of this being done systematically is the British Council's *Connecting Futures* programme, a new 5 year initiative which aims at building deeper mutual understanding, learning and respect between young people from different cultural backgrounds, by working in new ways and with wider, more diverse communities in the UK and overseas. The countries initially involved include Pakistan, Bangladesh, Malaysia, Indonesia, Saudi Arabia, Iran, Egypt, Turkey, Nigeria, the Palestinian Territories and the United Kingdom. *Connecting Futures* research has been carried out with five thousand young people aged 15-24 to find out their views of the UK and other countries and their own aspirations for the future. The idea is to use this research to develop new ways of working and engaging with a wider audience of young people using the internet and new communications technologies; through education, arts, sports and science projects; via school links and youth exchanges; by networking young professionals; by providing opportunities for open dialogue and debate; and by widening access to our information and education services.

The second problem is that a **one-way flow of messages** is likely to be counter-productive. A major source of difficultly for the positive presentation of Western countries abroad is the widespread anger at what is perceived to be a one-way flow of culture from the West to the rest of the world. The perception that local customs, local histories and local identities are being hollowed out by the unstoppable advance of Gap, Starbucks, Tom Cruise and *Who Wants to be a Millionaire?*, although it may not be true, is certainly damaging. It risks creating an adversarial attitude between 'the West and the Rest'.

In many countries there is also a post-imperial sensitivity toward the actions and messages of the UK. Rebuttal of arguments about neo-colonialism – although vital in the short term – can in the long term only lead to a 'dialogue of the deaf' unless real relationships that are seen to be mutual can be developed.

In order to avoid impotent argument falling on deaf ears it is important to have the right message and the right positioning on a topic. We can learn from the recent repositioning of French public diplomacy, which used to be based on pushing French cultural exceptionalism and promoting the French language. With the creation of their new department for public diplomacy,

DGCID, they set out a new mission for the organisation: instead of seeking to promote French exceptionalism, it sought common cause with other countries on the receiving end of US cultural dominance and positioned itself as the champion of those countries that felt swamped. In a similar manoeuvre, when it became apparent that French could not compete with English as a global language, they sought to promote *multi*lingualism: if French were not to be the first foreign language learned around the world, it was important to try and ensure that more than one foreign language would be learned.

This means pushing pluralism as a central part of the UK's culture and identity, and emphasising the impact that foreign cultures have in Britain. One example of an institution that is very effective at building such mutuality into Britain's relations with other countries is Visiting Arts. By bringing artists and performers from other cultures over to Britain, they present a very positive image of a receptive British culture that plays well in the proud originating country and works well to dispel concerns about cultural hegemony or a dominating attitude from the UK toward the third world. Yet the budget of Visiting Arts is tiny compared to the amount of money spent disseminating British cultural products through the British Council – the Arts department's budget is close to £21 million pounds, and around £1 million is spent on Visiting Arts projects. The scope for improvement in this area is large, particularly in comparison to the French model of budgeting, which has a pot of money allocated to each country for cultural exchange in general, which is then spent on facilitating a two-way cultural flow.

One other idea for promoting mutuality in relations with other countries is to emphasise the utility of working closely with institutions in that country to carry out simultaneous mutually beneficial public diplomacy. Close co-ordination between, say, the UK and German governments on the negative aspects of their respective national images would, in the first place obviously address those particular image problems, but more broadly serve as excellent public diplomacy *about* that public diplomacy. The British Council and the Goethe Institute in Germany are currently planning activities along these lines, to be preceded by a reciprocal research project. If the activity seems to be coming from a standpoint of mutual interest, rather than of promotional work by one country in another, then it will have greater impact and be treated with less suspicion on both sides.

In a similar vein, the World Service is looking to expand its role as a forum for debate, moving toward greater interactivity and involvement of it audiences. The World Service has already had success in the 'Talking Point' combined radio and online programme which engages audiences in discussions with world leaders and with each other. For example, after September 11th a special edition of the programme received some 30,000 e-mails from eyewitnesses and people who wanted to express their feelings about the events.

The third challenge is to **move beyond intellectual forms of communication**. Recent advertisements for the Morgan Stanley Dean Witter credit card hold that 93 per cent of all communication is non-verbal. While it is difficult to trust their exact figure, it is clear that many other factors – experience, emotions, images – will influence people's response to our messages. The challenge is to move from supplying information to capturing the imagination.

The British Ambassador to Washington, Sir Christopher Meyer, explained the importance of symbolism in Washington after September 11: "The British stock has never been higher in the

US. It is a combination of words and symbols – at three events. First, Blair saying "it is an attack on us all." Then on September 13th the playing of the star-spangled banner at the changing of the guard at Buckingham Palace. And third, when the President made his address to congress, there was Blair up in the Gallery showing his support. The combination of these events produced a surge of affection for the UK. What we are really saying to Americans is that we are the only people in the entire cosmos who you can really count on when the going gets tough."

Lury and Gibson point out that "more people understand fox-hunting as a result of listening to the Archers than from listening to endless pro and anti debates. An episode of Eastenders or Brookside or Coronation Street will do more to change people's attitude towards race or homosexuality or crime than all the work of think tanks put together". There are ways of projecting an image which either changes or reinforces the way people think through the provision of information – but we must constantly examine the forms and content of our different types of communication if we are going to capture people's imaginations.

For example, one of the most successful humanitarian operations in Afghanistan, UNICEF's inoculation of 7 million children in just 3 weeks, was only made possible by the extremely effective dissemination of information about the importance and purpose of inoculation through a popular soap opera on the BBC's Pashtun service. This dramatisation of important issues is an excellent way of communicating with broad populations, and has also been employed to put across messages about HIV and Aids in Vietnam, and conflict prevention in Indonesia.

The fourth challenge is **proving your relevance**. For many people around the world, it is no longer a given that a country like the United Kingdom matters. All the survey data shows that people in many countries see the UK as country in decline. In the first British Council *Through Other Eyes* survey 'Tradition/conservatism/stasis' was the most common unprompted suggestion of the UK's major weakness (with 11 per cent), whilst Northern Ireland came second with 5 per cent. In the follow-up survey, conservatism was still top, with 19 per cent. This also comes out from focus groups. One young professional in India said of the British: "They don't realise that the British Empire is no longer there. They still cannot digest this fact that [they] are not the best. So it will still take some time for them to come out of their shell and start competing with the rest of the world." This is echoed in a focus group response for Spain (from *Through Other Eyes* 2): "They are living in the past. They still think that they are the best, but they haven't been the best for fifty years and they don't know."

This means that in many countries where perceptions of the UK are positive, people do not see it as a significant partner. For example in Poland our focus groups showed that though young people were more favourable to Britain, they would all turn to Germany as a natural partner in the EU accession process as a result of their perceptions of the relative influence of Germany in the EU system (see Poland case study in Appendix I). Proving our relevance should not take the form of protestations in speeches and promotional literature. There is sometimes a tendency to believe that by asserting that we are the 4th largest economy in the world, members of the UN Security Council, leading players in Europe, etc, we are demonstrating our relevance. The challenge is to understand the concerns of the target audience and build on areas of mutuality, while making the most of actual British successes to show that we are relevant through our actions.

One way of proving one's relevance is to concentrate on 'niche diplomacy'. Norway is a good example of a country that has a voice and presence on the international stage out of proportion to its modest position and unpromising assets. It has achieved this presence through a ruthless prioritisation of its target audiences and its concentration on a single message – Norway as a force for peace in the world. Positioning as a contributor to world peace enables Norway to achieve greater visibility than its size would otherwise warrant and rebuts accusations of isolationism. Main activities in this field are conflict resolution activity in the Middle East (the Oslo Accords) Sri Lanka and Colombia, and Norway's large aid budget. Norway also operates a 'rapid-reaction force' to assist in election monitoring and conflict prevention – The Norwegian Resource Bank for Democracy and Human Rights (NORDEM) – that manages to operate in around 20 countries annually. The closeness of NORDEM's co-operation with OSCE further emphasises Norway's contribution to peace with key allies. The Nobel Peace Prize originating in Oslo is a happy historical fact which gives Norway a widely recognised peg to hang this side of its story on. (See Appendix II.)

But this approach of demand-led niche diplomacy needs to go beyond strategic messages – it must be reflected in all activities. A senior official in the British Council makes this point effectively: "In our experience you can only build relationships by tapping into people's needs. You can't engage them meaningfully – i.e. beyond the cocktail chat – in any other way. That's why we market English classes to targets (as a foot in the door), design seminars and other colloquia around practical issues rather than philosophical debate, and develop alumni groups around professional needs rather than just social circuitry."

6. Diplomacy by stealth:
Working with others to achieve our goals

Trust is essential for effective public diplomacy, and yet, for a series of reasons, foreign governments find it increasingly hard to gain. Some difficulties are structural, to do with the natural assumption that a gap exists between the interests of one country and another (if a message is delivered from a conspicuously 'British' standpoint, or appear to be 'the Voice of America', it will arouse suspicions of partisanship). Some difficulties are a result of the way in which all institutions, and particularly government institutions, are facing increasing public scepticism (In Britain opinion polls by MORI suggest that politicians and government ministers are trusted by only 20 per cent of the population, compared to doctors at 91 per cent, TV newsreaders at 71 per cent and even 'the Ordinary Man in the Street' at 54 per cent). The situation is even more complex in countries with totalitarian governments. Other problems are specific to the public diplomacy of Western countries and governments, and linked to prevailing issues of international power structures and geopolitical history. Consequently, obstacles for effectively putting across a message to a foreign population layer on top of one another, making the job of public diplomacy increasingly complicated. This raft of problems cannot be easily circumvented. They can, however, be alleviated; and central strategies for doing that involve working locally, a commitment to independence, a focus on mutuality, and an awareness of positioning.

The traditional approach to public diplomacy activity overseas, be it cultural festivals, seminars, economic promotion or policy advocacy, is that it should all be topped and tailed with "a few words from the Ambassador." In fact it would be far more useful in many cases to keep British governmental involvement with an event as inconspicuous as possible. Where possible messages should be disseminated by people with something in common with the target audience – Raymond Blanc made a far more convincing advocate for the safety and quality of British beef in France than the agricultural attaché at the embassy, or the Ambassador himself. And the decision to arrange visits of prominent Muslims living in Britain to Islamic countries in the wake of the 11 September was a more convincing demonstration of British respect for Islam than ministerial pronouncements.

The general lesson is that if a message will attract distrust simply because it is perceived to be coming from a foreign government, make sure it appears to be coming from a foreign government as little as possible. Increasingly, in order for a state to have its voice heard, and to have influence on events outside its direct control, it must work through organisations and networks that are separate from, independent of, and even culturally suspicious toward government itself. The contribution of NGOs to the push for restrictions on the use of landmines, for example, demonstrates the potential benefits that can come from partnerships with such groups. Similar benefits could equally come from working more closely with foreign political parties, harnessing the power of brands, or from realising the potential inherent in the growing diaspora that have accompanied the increasing incidence of migration. Yet in order for such potential leverage to be well employed, governments must exhibit sensitivity to the peculiar circumstances that surround any such alliance, and must be aware of the kinds of pitfalls that may accompany it.

NGO Diplomacy
Working with non-state actors such as NGOs is central to effective communication with civil societies in other countries (and hence central to influencing their governments) because

they have three key resources that are not necessarily easily available to a foreign government: credibility, expertise, and appropriate networks. Whilst people are often quick to question the motivations behind the diplomatic pronouncements of a state or suspicious of information relayed directly by a government, NGOs like Amnesty or Oxfam have a long-standing reputation for independence – and hence a credibility – that it is not feasible for a government to build up itself. The Environics International Global Issues survey of 1000 people in each of the G 20 countries found that 65 per cent of people said that they trusted NGOs to work in the best interests of society, compared to only 45 per cent trusting national governments to do the same.

Secondly, these organisations possess great expertise within a range of issues which, coupled with their reputation for independence, gives them authority. Lastly, as campaigning organisations as well as centres of expertise, they have access to networks of activists, experts and foreign politicians and are experienced at marshalling those networks to exert pressure in a given policy area. No diplomatic mission possesses (or would wish to possess) the capability to organise demonstrations on the streets, nor are they well positioned to co-ordinate sustained lobbying campaigns. There are over 20,000 transnational NGO networks already active on the world stage (of which 90 per cent were formed during the last 30 years) many of whom could make effective partners for the conduct of public diplomacy. There are already examples of the Foreign Office seconding and then permanently taking on employees of certain environmental NGOs, people from Amnesty International in its human rights sections, and even recruiting its Head of Policy Planning from Oxfam, but co-operation on an organisational level could be even more fruitful.

It is important, however, to be clear-eyed about such relationships, as they bring their own peculiar difficulties. In forming alliances with the non-state sector, government would essentially be seeking to exploit synergies between its own agenda and that of independent people or organisations that could be more or less great, and extend to broader or narrower policy areas. The obvious corollary of this is that government must be more relaxed about deviations from the 'party line' between itself and its partners in areas that are peripheral, and it should be prepared to accept the necessary relinquishment of control that would go with such an alliance. Equally, the government side must be aware of the impact of differences in organisational culture with the NGO sector; NGOs have a much more informal culture, and tend to work on a 'want-to-know' rather than a 'need-to-know' basis. Government has to be prepared to accept the impact these differences have on working practices and on information dispersal within a given project.

There have been several notable successes that have come out of government co-operation with the non-state sector. For example, the problem of 'conflict diamonds' being smuggled on to the world market, and consequently funding some of Africa's bloodiest civil wars in Sierra Leone, Angola and Liberia, could not have been effectively tackled without sustained government action alongside NGOs and business. Sovereign governments, including the UK and Canada, acted to bring together representatives from the diamond industry, particularly De Beers and the World Diamond Council, and NGOs like Global Witness and Human Rights Watch in the ongoing 'Kimberly Process', under the aegis of the UN. The resulting steps taken to regulate international diamond trade and to seek to ensure that no diamond money found its way back into conflict zones could only have been carried out by such a coalition.

Another example of synergies between government desires and capabilities and those of the NGO sector bringing some success is the Jubilee 2000 process. The organisation of a successful campaign of debt relief faced two structural problems: in the first place the key institutional mover, the G7/8, lacked any institutional continuity; and in the second place, debt relief as a political issue was of low salience for governments. In essence, fine words at G7 summits could not be translated directly into action as the G7 lacks any kind of bureaucracy or administrative capacity. Equally, it was also difficult to persuade governments to act, as debt relief was not a bread and butter issue for any significant proportion of their electorates, and presented in the short term only visible costs, without concrete benefits. However, an informal coalition of a Gordon Brown/Claire Short axis in the British Cabinet and a coterie of campaigning NGOs was able to launch an effective process at the Birmingham summit in 1998. Government provided the institutional continuity that was lacking, whilst the NGO sector was able to exploit its resources and expertise to keep the issue high on political agendas.

One final, famous, example is the highly successful campaign to eradicate the use of landmines worldwide. In a strikingly successful piece of non-state based diplomacy, the Canadian and Norwegian governments were able to ally themselves with several anti-landmine NGOs and together place a landmine ban formally on international agendas, whilst campaigning successfully to raise the profile of the issue informally. The result was the establishment of a new international norm through skilled diplomatic exploitation of a synergy between government and non-government sections of global civil society.

The opportunities for advantageous relations with the non-state sector are also more numerous and easier to grasp for the UK because of the large number of world class NGOs with headquarters in the UK. Examples include Oxfam, Amnesty International, Save the Children and Action Aid. Whilst the government has made efforts to include NGOs in its decision-making and build broader links with them, much more could be done. One idea would be to formalise relations through sending representatives to some of these NGOs – thus allowing a continuity of contact and the capability for swifter reaction if it were needed.

Diaspora Diplomacy

One of the central features of the increased volume of international migration in the latter half of the twentieth century is that there now exist 'living links' – relations, friends, former business partners – with virtually every country in the world. One striking measure of this is that London is one of the world's most linguistically mixed cities, where over 300 languages are in everyday use.

There have been attempts to tap in to and strengthen the diplomatic potential which those links represent. One example is the British Council's 'Connecting Futures' project (mentioned above) which, in the aftermath of September 11th, seeks to bring together young people from ethnic minority groups in the UK with young people from Muslim countries from Nigeria to Egypt and Indonesia and attempt to improve their mutual understanding. Another example is the Foreign Office's high profile dispatch of a consulate team to the Muslim pilgrimage, the Hajj, which was intended both to provide assistance to the 20,000 British Muslims who perform the Hajj, and as an initiative in cultural relations. The British Council in India has also instituted an innovative programme of events and activities that shows the contribution of the diaspora to UK culture and business.

The untapped potential in the UK diaspora could, with sustained involvement, yield several advantages to UK foreign policy. Firstly, and most obviously, it can help fill the demand for language skills that has been highlighted by the events following September 11th, where Pashtun, Farsi and Arabic speakers were much sought after. A similar shock from elsewhere in the world would make similar demands.

Furthermore, such links undoubtedly help provide the cultural knowledge, political insight and human intelligence that is necessary for successful foreign policy. It has often been observed, for instance, that the mistakes and unpleasant surprises that mark the history of events like the Vietnam War or the Iranian Revolution might have been avoided had there been more comprehensive and intimate knowledge of those societies available to policy-makers. Daniel Ellsberg, the Department of Defense official who leaked the Pentagon Papers on US decision-making in Vietnam, has for instance laid great emphasis on what he asserts is a fact that no official in the US administration at the time of the war's escalation "could have passed a mid-term paper in Vietnamese History". The thickness of relations that the UK's thriving diaspora represent should be a great advantage in reducing misapprehensions of other societies.

There are also important economic benefits to be had by focusing on the diaspora as a channel of public diplomacy: tourism, trade, investment, skills. James Rauch of the University of California, San Diego, has argued that over time a 10 per cent increase in immigrants to the US will increase US exports to the country of origin by 4.7 per cent and US imports from the country of origin by 8.3 per cent. Professor Rauch also reports that in Canada a 10 per cent increase in immigrants from a given country eventually increases Canadian exports to that country by 1.3 per cent and imports from there by 3.3 per cent".

Lastly, the nurturing of talent from those diaspora not only provides government with representatives who are sensitive to, and possess credibility with, foreign populations, it also is excellent public diplomacy itself for attracting further talent from those countries to the UK. It is a measure of how far there is to come in this regard (and consequently of what potential lies untapped) that there is, as yet, no one from an ethnic minority in the upper echelons of the Foreign and Commonwealth Office, British Council, TPUK, or Invest UK – and only a handful of individuals on middle management.

There are, however, dangers and caveats which must be borne in mind in public diplomacy dealings with diaspora. The first cautionary tale to be aware of is the history of the capture of aspects of US foreign policy by ethnic groups, preventing the US government taking action which otherwise it would consider to be the most advantageous. There have been some signs that similar ethnic interests have taken over some sections of local politics in the UK – it is, for instance, not a healthy effect of such diaspora politics that local government elections in Bradford can concentrate on problems in Kashmir, rather than in West Yorkshire.

A second important, and easily overlooked, aspect of this is the complexity of relations between different diaspora of the same country. A focus group we organised with young professionals in Delhi revealed very different attitudes toward the Indian diaspora in the US and the UK. Indians in the UK are commonly seen as low-skilled, low wage, and non-aspirational – an image essentially dominated by the corner shop and the import-export trade. In stark contrast the US Indian diaspora is seen in a very positive light, as ambitious and highly skilled – an image heavily influenced by the perceived prevalence of Indians in the IT industry in Silicon Valley (see India case study, Appendix I). One respondent said: "I think that the community in the UK are traders, merchants, and businessmen. They are not professionals (if you don't include doctors). In the US Indian's are the smart set and that sort of perception generates a certain amount of affinity and warmth, which in the current situation is not there between the Indians and the English". The conclusion that should be drawn from this differentiation is that attention should be paid to improving the image, not just of the UK generally, but of specific diaspora within it if their full potential is to be utilised.

Lastly, there is a considerable danger that government relations with the UK diaspora become captured by stereotypes or over-concentrate on traditionally defined "community leaders". There is a significant risk that conceptions of dealing with diaspora become racialised, and concentrate largely on links between non-white ethnic groups. If this were allowed to happen then the equally advantageous links that could be developed with, for example, the significant UK Polish diaspora, or those of Australia or the US, might be overlooked. Linked to this is the danger that the government seek to communicate with such communities through their self-appointed leaders. To do this is to damagingly homogenise an ethnic group into a small coterie of generally male, middle-aged representatives. In order for public diplomacy through the diaspora to be effective it must instead take in and seek to employ the full diversity of that ethnic group.

Political Party Diplomacy

A third area where non-government to government diplomacy could be very fruitful is in building relations between political parties of different countries. Many problems between governments that superficially appear to be diplomatic are, unavoidably, difficulties that revolve around perceived political differences. For example, one important contributing factor to the frosty relations that have sometimes prevailed between Britain and France in the last few years has been the suspicion is some parts of the French left toward New Labour's perceived neo-liberal standpoint.

Sir Michael Jay, the permanent Under Secretary at the Foreign Office and former Ambassador to Paris explains: "The French perception of Blairite liberalism as being 'Ultimate Liberalism' without any concern for social infrastructure got very much in the way of persuading the French to adopt a liberalising agenda in the EU. People who didn't want to listen to these things fell back on the stereotypes of railways not working and NHS waiting lists. What gets across in France is that this is what happens if you follow British policies – rather than the fact that these are real problems that that an imaginative and energetic government is committed to solving in an innovative way….In this sense economic and social misconceptions are more unhelpful than cultural ones….There is a lot to be said for closer contact between political parties, but there are questions of clarity of objectives and monitoring that would need to be sorted out."

The relations between political parties of the same broad stripe in different countries can be a vitally important dimension of their overall foreign relations, and one that the United Kingdom has been very poor at managing because of its overemphasis on a structure of diplomacy based on states.

Britain has long been suspicious of mixing politics and diplomacy. It's vision of diplomacy is heavily influenced by the Palmerstonian outlook of the mid-nineteenth century: what international relations scholars refer to as 'realism'. This approach, which imagines that political ideas and politicians may come and go, but the interests of Britain remain eternal, is ever more discredited in an interdependent world. On a growing list of issues – economic reform, social rights, agriculture, drugs, terrorism, the environment, humanitarian intervention – Britain's interests are neither immutable, nor particular to Britain alone. Instead, such issues can only be dealt with through a deliberative political process. Increased links between political parties, especially within the EU countries, represent one way to deal with that historic shift, and the UK's outdated idea of the political independence of diplomacy can only serve to cripple us in that new environment.

Other countries have been prepared to foster such relations. One example is Germany's Konrad Adenhauer Stiftung and Freidrich Ebert Stiftung – large, politically oriented institutes that receive substantial amounts of state funding to facilitate policy debate and exchange between different countries (see box overleaf). The advantages which such efforts produce can be placed under three headings. Firstly, by nurturing relations between the politicians of different countries, it makes diplomacy easier by giving both sides a clear idea of the political positioning and possibilities of the other. Secondly it allows a channel for policy exchange that represents the infrastructure required to renew the intellectual capital of political parties, and for bringing in new ideas to debate. Thirdly, it helps develop an international outlook within parties that are not at that time in government that can be very advantageous in smoothing transition between administrations. It is interesting to note that the only UK budget available for activities remotely similar to that of the German Stiftungen is through the Westminster Foundation for Democracy, and is therefore only available in transition countries. As soon the transition to a democratic civil society begins to present the desired opportunities for closer co-operation, the infrastructure for capitalising on those links disappears.

But it is important to recognise that there will need to be clear safe-guards to ensure that the activities promoted are appropriate. It would be tremendously damaging for a government to use its resources and position on the international stage to secure party political capital for itself.

Improving links between political parties would also not necessarily involve the sizeable bureaucracy and considerable expense of the German Stiftung system. (The Friedrich Ebert Stiftung alone has an annual budget of DM 204 million, distributed to over 90 countries.) Instead, it would be much more practical to expand the British Council's remit into a policy exchange role - particularly within the other EU countries where such political links are most vital. Alternatively, a desk officer, seconded from each of the three main political parties, could be seconded to the British Council or embassy in each EU country with a remit to foster cross-border party relations. In either case the central point is that political parties should be treated in the same way as other NGOs, and provided with funds to develop international networks that are advantageous to the UK in a similar way to those of Oxfam or Amnesty.

Brand Diplomacy
Over the last twenty years brands have become one of the most important channels for transmitting national identities to consumers. Whereas earlier generations may have identified countries primarily through their history, political institutions or high culture, today brands can form an important part of the national image of some countries. Some brands such as Coca Cola or Levi's have always derived much of their emotive pull from associations with the American way of life, its values and freedom. But in many situations this formula is reversed. Very

The German Stiftungen

The Friedrich-Ebert-Stiftung

The Freidrich-Ebert-Stiftung has a threefold aim: furthering a democratic, pluralistic political culture through political education; facilitating access to higher education by providing scholarships to young people; and contributing to international understanding and co-operation wherever possible "to avert a fresh outbreak of war and conflict."

The Stiftung has a total of 581 staff in the head office in Bonn, the six educational centres, the twelve regional offices and abroad. It has offices in 90 countries and is active in more than 100. Its activities include political education within Germany and the award of scholarships (1700 scholarships were awarded in 2000, 340 of those to foreign nationals.) Internationally, it is involved in projects in the fields of economic and social development, socio-political education and information, the media and communication and providing advisory services. Approximately half of the Foundation's annual budget is devoted to this co-operation with partners in the trade unions, politics, the business and academic communities, the media and the arts. Its aims are differentiated between developing and industrialised countries.

In developing countries it works toward: the improvement of political and social framework conditions; the democratisation of social structures; the strengthening of free trade unions; the improvement of communication and media structures; regional and international media co-operation;regional co-operation between states and different interest groups; and overcoming the North-South conflict.

In industrialised countries the Friedrich-Ebert-Stiftung seeks to "foster dialogue amongst all democratic forces with the aim of bringing about a balance of interests, solving conflicts and developing policy options." In transitional countries particularly in Eastern Europe the Friedrich-Ebert-Stiftung is involved in supporting the transition to a market economy and establishing a civil society, particularly in the fields of labour market, social, environmental and media policy. It has a budget of approximately 204 million DM (in 2000); coming mainly from central and regional government funding.

The Konrad Adenauer Stiftung

The Konrad-Adenauer-Stiftung is affiliated to the Christian Democratic movement, and emerged from the 'Society for Christian Democratic Education Work' founded in 1956. It was named after the first Chancellor of the Federal Republic in 1964.

At present, it operates over 200 projects and programmes in more than 100 countries. It has a budget of DM 200m of which more than DM 100m is earmarked for international activities. It is funded by the Federal Ministry for Economic Cooperation and Development as well as by the Foreign Office.

It works with foreign political parties, parliaments and governments; education and research institutes; universities; industry confederations and trade unions; cooperative societies; women's, environmental, and self-help organisations; and the media.

Its activities include:

- political education (Only in Germany)
- conduct of scientific and fact-finding research for political projects
- scholarship grants
- research into the history of Christian Democracy
- support and encouragement for European unification, international understanding, and development-policy cooperation.

few people have been to Japan or Sweden, but they have very powerful associations with these countries through their purchases of branded products – whether it is perceptions of technological sophistication in Sony, Nintendo or Tamagoshis, or design simplicity through IKEA, Saab and Ericsson.

This is because, as Wally Olins has argued, "Brands have become highly visible objects of consumption which have become a significant focus for the individual's loyalties. Global brands, some mass market like Nike, Coca-Cola, Burger King, others expensive like Prada, Gucci and Hermes demonstrate the individual's need for self-definition. These global brands also provide the comfort of representing an idea – youth, energy, good taste, money and so on. Individuals from every nation seem to be susceptible to this extraordinary phenomenon. While brand loyalty is no substitute for nationality, it certainly complements it".

The branding consultancy Interbrand has developed a methodology to measure the value of global brands and regularly produces a league table. The latest figures show the enormous discrepancy between the strength of different countries' brands. Over two thirds of brands (68 per cent) worth over $1 billion are American while no other country accounts for more than 6 per cent of brands. In fact Coca-Cola alone is worth as much as the combined brands of any other country. Britain comes second to the United States with 6 per cent, but its high valued brands (Unilever and Diageo) are involved in alcohol and mundane household products. These figures show the total dominance of the US and provide yet another clue to the US's dominant place in people's perceptions, but they only tell part of the story as they are based on the market capitalisation of the brands. In fact some of the British brands with the most resonance are not companies. For example the BBC brand has one of the highest recognitions in the world, and it is the only internet brand that trades globally in the same league as Yahoo, Google, MSN or AOL.

This relationship between brands and national perceptions is powerful and complex. Simon Anholt is one of many authors who have pointed out that the dominant perceptions which some of these national images create make it very difficult for 'non-typical' companies to promote themselves. This is the experience of the Italian Olivetti, who struggled against the dominant perceptions of Italy as a fashion or style producer or the German company Hugo Boss who feel constrained by the antisceptic images of German engineering and technical efficiency. Perhaps the decision of British-based consumer

Image 2: Brand Value Distributed by Country

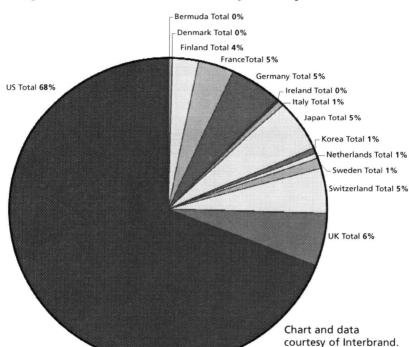

Chart and data courtesy of Interbrand. For table of data see Appendix III

electronics chain Dixons to call their own-brand products Matsui (and thus take on the persona of a Japanese company) is the best example of this clash taking place. It is for this reason that the main brands that have wanted to associate themselves with Britishness have been premium brands that trade on heritage such as Asprey's or Jaguar, who have formed an informal grouping called the Walpole Group which organises activities to promote traditional perceptions of Britain and explores how these different brands can exploit synergies in their respective markets.

This means that although businesses and their brands are an important part of the UK's face in many parts of the world, it is difficult to enlist their resources to change perceptions of the United Kingdom. Most businesses do not see promoting Britain as their responsibility either because they prefer not to be seen as British companies, or they do not see it as their job. But although many companies are striving to transcend their national identities and become 'global brands', very few have achieved this in practice – they are often seen in the phrase of Brian Boylan from Wolff Olins as being "global from somewhere". Research by BMP shows that whatever their aspirations, they are likely to be constrained by the advantages or disadvantages of national stereotypes for different sectors of the economy.

The failure to involve business successfully in national promotion has been threefold. First, it has been difficult to persuade more than a small number of very obviously British companies (such as British Airways) that perceptions of Britain are anything more than of marginal importance to them. Secondly, businesses have been wary of getting caught up in a controversial political project like 'Cool Britannia'. And thirdly, it has been seen as a government scheme to get money out of companies, rather than a strategic use of their assets to improve their market position and the national brand.

If this situation is to be turned round, new initiatives will need to be seen to start with business priorities rather than governments, and business must be in the driving seat. In the long-term, it would be positive for a group of modern, aspirational companies such as Virgin, Psion, Dyson or Channel 4 to organise promotional campaigns that showcase a modern dynamic Britain, in the same way that the Walpole Group reflects the British heritage brand. The result could be similar to the situation in Japan where its reputation as a producer of high-quality consumer goods has not displaced the traditional images of nature, geisha girls and cherry blossom still used by the Japan Tourist Office alongside more modern images. However, a shift has taken place in people's 'top of mind' picture of Japan, which is predominantly contemporary, compared with the UK's, where it is predominantly traditional. The challenge is to reinforce contemporary images of the UK to move the balance of young people's 'top of mind' image.

But in the short-term, it is probably more sensible to begin with a manageable project which is evidently in the interests of all big companies in Britain. One solution which has been proposed by the management consultants McKinseys is the idea of organising a campaign designed to attract talent to Britain. Talent is increasingly mobile despite immigration restrictions – looking for the best opportunities and lifestyles it can find in the world. In Silicon Valley it is estimated that 15 per cent of successful entrepreneurs are first generation Indian immigrants. London already has a good story to tell on the bread and butter issues of political freedom, gender equality, education, tax and legal systems which means the battle for skills is in the softer, more cultural territory. It lays claim to huge strengths in its location (Europe), language (English), time zone (half-way between New York and Tokyo), social infrastructure and academic/creative excellence. This accounts for the fact that it is already the most popular location for European companies headquarters (with 107 compared to 37 in Paris, 14 in Brussels and 10 in Frankfurt). These companies should be targeted for support on an aggressive campaign including prizes at top business, creative and scientific institutions around the world. This ties in with the recent announcement by the Home Secretary David Blunkett to double the number of work permits for highly skilled workers, which presents an obvious and legitimate opportunity for a business-led campaign in this area.

7: Good Practice and Gaps in the Spectrum of British Institutions

Britain has some of the most effective and envied public diplomacy institutions around the world. The BBC World Service consistently outperforms all its rivals in terms of reach, impact and reputation. The British Council has built on its strong identity with wide-ranging reforms carried out in recent years that have been seen as a model by the French, German and Norwegian Governments in their recent reviews of cultural relations. Invest UK has overseen consistently higher levels of inward investment than any other EU country. And there are an array of other institutions from TPUK and the British Tourist Authority to the Westminster Foundation for Democracy and DFID whose work around the world brings benefit to the UK.

And yet the whole of this spectrum of institutions and activities remains less than the sum of its parts. Despite all the talk of 'joined-up government', 'strategic co-ordination', and the establishment of various reviews of UK public diplomacy, there is still no overarching strategy to ensure that we are promoting the right messages and spanning the three dimensions of public diplomacy. The table below shows that there are some major gaps which are not adequately covered by the institutions at our disposal. In this chapter, we will examine the institutions as a spectrum and see whether there are gaps between them which are not yet filled. We have divided our assessment of the spectrum of institutions under four headings: the three dimensions of public diplomacy; strategic co-ordination and planning; differentiation; and evaluation.

Table 3: How do British Institutions Span the Three Dimensions of Public Diplomacy?

Purpose	Reactive	Proactive	Relationship building
Political/Military	GOOD at post level. MIXED work with London-based correspondents.	GAP on promotion of strategic messages, though some single issues campaigns.	MIXED. Some good initiatives British Council and Embassies, but no strategy to work with political parties. Danger of Gap emerging as opinion-makers increasingly turn from radio to TV.
Economic	GOOD at post level. MIXED work with London-based correspondents.	GAP on general promotion. GOOD with specialist audiences.	GOOD work by Invest UK and TPUK.
Society/Culture	GOOD at post level. MIXED work with London-based correspondents.	GAP on popular culture. GOOD. British Council on arts events.	GOOD. British Council with professional groups. BBC reaches wider audience.

The Three Dimensions

We argue that we need a clearer distribution of responsibility according to the dimensions rather than subject matter. It is clear that the FCO needs to be the lead institution on news management, with the FCO, British Council and World Service leading on political and cultural relationship-building and TPUK playing that role in the economic sphere. For strategic communications, the FCO, British Council, TPUK and Invest UK all need to devote more resources in all three spheres.

News Management

The official government structures that are in place for dealing with the media were devised before the era of globalisation and the 24-hour global news-cycle. Most embassies do an excellent job of responding to issues as they arise at country level, but they are not able to deal with many stories because they are in the wrong place. Reporting from posts in Europe and North America suggests that the most important source of stories about Britain are written by the 1,700 London-based foreign correspondents.

While the Foreign and Commonwealth Office's News Department will talk to the press about 'foreign' news stories, they will refer enquiries about domestic stories to the relevant departments. But the press offices of the Department of Transport or the Home Office are not equipped to understand the international repercussions of their actions. When they are going through a crisis, they will naturally be primarily concerned about domestic press coverage. Foreign correspondents (sometimes jokingly referred to by press officers in domestic departments as 'no votes TV') will inevitably get a second class service – struggling to get access to ministers, information and assistance.

Our research also found that press and public affairs officers in several British embassies have had difficulty getting clear information out of domestic departments. One official complained: "The lines MAFF produced may have been fine in the UK but they failed to address concerns overseas. The 'formal' end of foot and mouth was announced at midnight with no notice to embassies and no apparent discussion between DEFRA and FCO about how to deal with it in public diplomacy terms."

Because there is so little access to Government sources many foreign correspondents will rely on domestic media as a source for their stories. This means that foreign coverage of the UK often repeats the sensationalist accounts of the UK media – without giving the context which people in the country know through experience. It is therefore not uncommon for Britain to be described as 'a third world country' with a crumbling infrastructure – accepted as rhetoric by the domestic British audience, but easy to take out of context in the foreign press.

Things have got better since September 11th, but Alastair Campbell admits that there is still a long way to go: "We haven't got brilliant links out to the foreign media. They are not as good as they should be. And the issue is time, or the lack of it. For all that people talk about my great army of spin-doctors and all the rest of it, we don't have that much in terms of actual resources. I'm doing a briefing next week with all the American correspondents, we do regular briefings with the Arab media at the moment. But to be frank that is likely to slip if the Middle East calms down a bit. And at another point, you will suddenly find that you are having to deal much more with the European London-based media."

There is clearly a need to have at the very least better co-ordination, but ideally also someone in each Government department who is responsible for dealing with the foreign media. There are also important questions about whether the Government Information and Communications Service should not be the source of press and public affairs officers in embassies around the world, and whether it might not be possible to develop a cadre of internationally-minded experts within the service.

Strategic communications
The biggest gap in the public diplomacy armoury is at the level of proactive communications – both in terms of activities and the platforms that are covered. In the economic sphere, proactive communications are largely restricted to trade fairs and promotional campaigns amongst specialist audiences. There is a better record at getting to broader audiences in the cultural sphere, with some British Council offices appointing public relations professionals and using exhibitions such as the Design

Council's 'Millennium Products' to generate positive stories about UK innovation and creativity. The fashion week in Delhi was a good example of prestige elite events being used to create a multiplier effect which ensured positive features about the UK over a number of months (see India case study, Appendix I). Other examples include the 'Typiquement British' festival of over 200 films at the Pompidou centre in Paris which attracted rave reviews and audiences of over 70,000. There is, however, a major gap in the use of popular culture to change perceptions of the United Kingdom, as the British Council's arts department concentrates on experimental or high brow art. This is worrying as British popular culture produces some of the most visible icons of the country who could be used as door-openers for other activities and messages. What is more the British Council's *Through Other Eyes* survey showed that although figures from British popular culture are among the most recognisable in the world, many people think they are American.

In the political sphere, things are even more patchy. Press and public affairs officers spend most of their time reacting to issues that come up or putting out the latest messages about individual policy areas. So far, proactive communications have been restricted to dealing with difficult issues such as the French beef ban, the MacBride legislation in the United States or the war against terrorism. The British Embassy in Paris organized an extremely effective campaign over BSE including outreach work with local and regional media, tours by British vets and chefs as well as events on CJD and food safety with the British Council (see Appendix I).

The Coalition Information Centre was an impressive innovation as it took the craft of strategic communications beyond domestic politics into foreign policy. The results were excellent, with consistent themes being brought out and attempts to create positive news stories by orchestrating events such as a football match involving British soldiers in Afghanistan and visits to London by Hamid Kharzai and Dick Cheney on the sixth-month anniversary of September 11th. This sort of forward planning and thinking should become more of a defining feature of the communication teams of the British missions abroad.

Part of the problem is that few of the resources available are used as part of a strategic effort. In London, the FCO's Public Diplomacy Department produces material for radio and television which is of questionable use. In particular it is questionable whether producing official government news feeds is a viable tool for influence – and there are very few attempts to track what use is made of them. While some of the feature programmes, such as a documentary on Muslims living in the UK, have a much clearer purpose, the majority of the output is not linked to clear political priorities. Embassies have claimed that the range of printed and audiovisual resources are often inappropriate: too generic to be relevant for a particular country, and only available in English. In addition, the reliance on printed publications distributed from a central source means that time-limited material – such as the monthly 'Snapshot UK' – may simply arrive too late to be useful. Above all the materials produced have the feel of 'official' information which undermines their credibility. The FCO is currently reviewing its publications strategy with the goal of moving towards shorter, more flexible web-friendly publications which posts can use as a template for local production for use on their websites, and its radio and TV outputs.

There are also some gaps in the British media presence. A survey of young professionals in 30 countries (*Through Other Eyes*, 1999 and 2000) showed that local media (particularly press and TV) are among the most powerful sources of information for many

**Table 4: Main
sources of
information
about the UK**

Word of mouth
Local press
National TV news
Books
BBC World (TV)
British press
Visiting the UK
Internet
International press
Films

people. These two are topped only by word of mouth as the main sources of information about the UK, and ahead of British press and TV.

Missing off the 'top ten' list altogether is radio, both local radio and international radio services such as the BBC World Service. These came fifteenth and eleventh in the survey respectively. Although still a major medium in less-developed countries, radio as a source of information and influence is increasingly losing out to television in more developed countries and among more elite members of society. For example the BBC World service reported a fall of 12 million listeners in India last year (see India case study, Appendix I). This fall is likely to be replicated elsewhere as international radio stations are increasingly caught in a pincer movement between the rise of cable and satellite television on the one hand and growing competition from quality local and regional radio services – often taking advantage of political liberalisation – on the other. Over the last few years the extent of this shift has been partially obscured by the BBC's prescient decision to build up an FM presence, which has led to record listenership figures of 150 million. The fact that the BBC was the first international broadcaster to spot this opportunity has given it an important 'first-mover advantage', but changing patterns of media consumption and increased competition mean that the rise will soon plateau, and the BBC will face a serious risk of a decline in radio listeners.

The *Through Other Eyes* data on information sources shows the importance of sustained investment in television and the Internet if British public diplomacy is going to keep abreast of the patterns of consumption of its target groups. The picture on the Internet is positive. The BBC's online presence is impressive and it manages to attract one of the largest audiences of any site in the world. The British Council has launched a series of popular sites including its LearnEnglish site which attracts over 100,000 visitors a month and its FootballCulture site which attracts 70,000. The i-UK Portal project linking the activities of the main public sector partners (going live from the second half of 2002) should make an important contribution to making UK organisations' websites more user-friendly.

However television is a growing gap. It is an anomaly in that the BBC World Service receives public funding to support its radio and internet platforms, but its global television channel is run on a commercial basis. There are a number of explanations for this. First, television is more expensive to produce than radio and online, so the tax-payer can get a better reach for every pound spent on each of those platforms. Secondly – as BBC World is beginning to prove – it is easier to produce a commercially viable service on television than on internet or radio. BBC World has managed to secure a strong position in some markets – it is now available 24 hours a day in 91 million households. Data for our case study countries shows that it reaches three times as many viewers as CNN in India (but only half as many as Star News); is on a par with CNN in Poland; and reaches 630,000 households each day and 2.9 million people each week in the United States. Thirdly, the Government has been reluctant to authorise public funds for BBC World on the grounds that it will distort the market and give BBC World an unfair advantage over commercial operations such as Sky News.

But because it has taken longer to develop and not received the same resources for distribution and marketing, it does not match CNN International's reach or ability to set the news agenda.

CNN International also boasts the world's most syndicated news service, providing video and audio reportage to more than 900 television stations and more than 1700 radio stations worldwide. It is currently launching language websites (including a German and Arabic site) in competition with some of the BBC's 42 language sites which it is aggressively pushing across platforms – outspending the BBC Arabic web-site on marketing by a factor of 10.

At the moment commercial pressures mean that BBC World is not always able to match the breadth of programming and distinctiveness of the BBC World Service (although its incorporation into a new global news division along with the BBC World Service could signal a richer editorial agenda). This will need to change before the Government considers giving it public funding, as it will have to prove that that funding seriously adds value. But in the medium term, it will be necessary to make this investment if the BBC is going to have the same impact on the global news agenda in a cable and satellite age as it did in the era of short-wave. The case for publicly funded television is not that it will replace radio or online provisions - it's that successful broadcasters need to be active across all platforms to match increasingly complex patterns of media consumption. The UK cannot afford to be shut out of one of the key elements of broadcast media. While BBC World can operate on a commercial basis in developed markets, it cannot do so in non revenue-generating markets, some of which are crucial to the UK's political interests. France has already realised the critical importance of television as a public diplomacy medium and provided public funding to TV5. This has allowed it to become the 3rd largest international network in the world, available in 130m homes despite the fact that it is broadcast in French and does not build on a powerful media brand like the BBC.

Relationship building

Relationship-building has been the bread-and-butter work of the British Council and BBC World Service for decades. The BBC has built up a loyal global following among opinion formers in developed countries and much broader groups in developing countries (60 million weekly listeners in Africa including half the population in Tanzania, one third in Rwanda and 45 per cent in Lagos). They have earned high levels of trust across continents. Their research among cosmopolitans shows 89 per cent of respondents in the US regard the World Service as a trustworthy source of information, with 85 per cent doing so in Lagos and 86 per cent in Karachi. The fact that so many opinion-formers get their international news from the BBC is a powerful way of dealing with 'cognitive dissonance' – the danger that our basic starting points are very different from those of people in other countries, and that consequently any dialogue just results in us talking past each other.

The British Council has developed relationships with arts administrators, scientists, civil servants, academics, teachers, journalists, policy advisers, and even military personnel through language tuition, training and capacity-building, arts projects, school exchanges, and managing the Chevening scholarships on behalf of the FCO. More could be done to build relationships with the 350,000 people who are taught English in British Council offices every year, and it should also be a priority to carry out clear profiling of the 800,000 people who take exams administered by the Council every year. Anecdotal evidence shows that these are all highly educated, skilled individuals who would make good targets for public diplomacy activity, and would be a natural target group for any campaign to attract skilled workers to the United Kingdom.

In 2001 some 40,000 UK people were involved in exchanges organised by the British Council (including 20,000 young people who went on Connect Youth exchanges around the world and 1800 modern language students who went overseas as teaching assistants). 2500 foreign students from 20 countries were posted as teaching assistants in UK schools. There is a strong case for examining the branding, follow-up and organisation of these teaching assistantships, school exchanges, and Scholarships. Research by the British Council on the Chevening scheme shows that people's initial impressions of the UK are not always positive. It is clear that British schemes do not have the same prestige as some rival schemes such as the Japanese JET programme, or the Fulbright scholarships. Part of the problem might simply be the fact that very few people even in Britain know what Chevening is, but it would also be worth examining whether we have the right mix between applications and nominations, how we use our alumni networks, and whether we should consider organizing a greater number of shorter exchanges – rather than year-long stints – in order to attract people at the top end of their careers. (Particularly as evaluation by the British Council of its intensive visits programmes suggests that they are very effective, in the short-term at least, at improving perceptions of the UK.)

In the economic sphere both TPUK and Invest UK nurture contacts through their overseas networks, and by putting people in touch with relevant businesses in the UK or overseas. Also the network of Chambers of Commerce organises a series of private-sector driven activities in different countries with variable results.

But although long-term relationships in the economic and cultural spheres are strong, there is only a patchy record in developing long-term political relationships. Some brilliant

Atlantic, Greenwich and City Fellowships

Established in 1994 to commemorate the 50th anniversary of D-Day and the US contribution to the liberation of Europe, the **Atlantic Fellowships in Public Policy** are intended to attract outstanding US mid-career professionals to spend time in the UK.

The Atlantic Fellowships have three main stated goals: enabling US public policy experts to benefit from British ideas and best practice, thus enhancing their ability to make contributions to policymaking in the US; share ideas on best practice in public policy for mutual benefit; and creating a transatlantic network of public policy experts and practitioners to encourage ongoing collaboration and exchange.

Around ten Fellowships are awarded annually, sponsored and funded by the FCO and administered by the British Council USA. Since 1994, 54 Fellowships have been awarded to professionals from public, business and philanthropic sectors for periods of between six and ten months.

Also set-up in 1994, the **City Fellowships Programme** brings young American financial services professionals from ethnic minorities to work in the City of London. The scheme is funded through banks and financial services firms like NatWest, Bank of Scotland, J.P. Morgan and Goldman Sachs. The total value of fellowships awarded to date is approximately $6 million.

The **Greenwich Fellowships in International Journalism**, established in 1999, are also aimed at ethnic minorities - this time in the field of journalism. Experienced American ethnic minority journalists are given the opportunity to work for a British news organisation while acting as a mentor to young British minority journalists for up to one year. The stated aims of the Greenwich Fellowships include strengthening the links between the United Kingdom and the ethnic minorities of the United States, and building professional relationships between journalists in Britain and the US.

initiatives are scattered around but there has been no systematic attempt to nurture these relationships. One of the main reasons is a culture which sees it as improper for British diplomacy to explicitly support political activities. While it would clearly be inappropriate for tax-payers' money to be expended on 'politicking' there are clearly a range of activities – around policy exchange, networking and debates about core values - which could play an important role in helping the UK promote its interests (see above, Chapter 6, on Political Party Diplomacy).

Embassies are constrained in this role as it is difficult for them to create a neutral space for people to meet informally, and in some countries it is awkward for them to bring together figures from across the political spectrum (See South Africa case study for an example of this; and of the corresponding increase in the importance of the British Council, Appendix I). Added to this is the fact that most embassies abroad lack the programme budgets, manpower and expertise to organise major events of this type. Nevertheless, some have created innovative programmes such as policy-maker exchanges (the Atlantic fellowships in Washington) and work with bilateral organisations (Konigswinter in Germany).

This is an area which the British Council is beginning to make its own. Bilateral events like UKUZA in South Africa, Pontignano in Italy, the Prague Castle Conference and the Anglo-Belgian forum are high-profile, high-calibre networking events which have become a feature in the political calendar of the countries concerned. The European Think Tank forum which brought together young policy-makers from around the European Union and many accession countries was a unique experiment in creating a multilateral debate on the future of the EU.

These events are incredibly useful but are slightly constrained by a narrow definition of political neutrality which insists they all bring together politicians from across the political spectrum and mix them with broader cultural figures and journalists in any single event rather than across a programme of activity. It might be worth changing the definition so that the equally useful activity of bringing together special advisers or ministers from the centre-left or centre-right from around Europe to talk about high salience issues like migration or health policy in separate groups might be undertaken.

There is a strong case for giving the British Council extra resources to fill this gap. It is currently not resourced to develop exciting political programmes in the way that it is to put together arts programmes. The Civil Society, Human Rights and Governance department only has 15 staff to cover the whole spectrum from capacity building in developing countries to policy exchange in EU countries, compared to the Arts Department's 100 staff. This will also require a cultural change in Embassies, who have jealously protected their role as gatekeepers to the political world – even if they have not invested the resources themselves in these activities.

Strategic Co-ordination
Though the independence of the British Council and World Service have been essential to their success, there is a danger of duplication and lack or co-ordination in the UK spectrum of public diplomacy institutions.

The BBC World Service, although almost entirely Government funded, has total editorial independence – unlike the Voice of America. This fact is recognised in almost every country in which it broadcasts, with the result that it is trusted as a media source more highly than the VOA. The British Council, as a non-governmental body, is able to work much more flexibly in some countries than embassies, which must maintain government to government links. In apartheid-era South Africa, the British Council worked entirely with non-government organisations, creating links with and earning the respect of those now in government (see the South Africa case study, Appendix I).

But on the downside, poor co-ordination between the different institutions can lead both to the gaps in the overall public diplomacy effort that we have discussed, and to duplication and wasted effort. For example:

- In some countries both the embassy and the British Council promote themselves as the leading source of general information about the UK.

- The FCO's Planet Britain and the British Council's CultureLab websites, both aimed at young people, were developed at the same time without any collaboration between the organisations.

Work has started on putting systems in place which will improve this situation. In the UK, a co-ordinating forum for sharing and agreeing the public diplomacy approaches of the different organisations has been set up but has yet to prove itself effective. A separate body, Britain Abroad, was set up in 2001 for the purpose of bringing together the various public sector organisations and companies with a stake in how the UK is perceived overseas. It has had some success in getting partners – both public and private sectors – to share experience and work more closely together in areas such as research, but its proposals for additional, focused public diplomacy activities have not so far been funded.

Overseas, embassies have set up public diplomacy committees with members from the embassy, the British Council, and, in some countries DFID, the British Tourist Authority and representatives of British companies. But the effectiveness of these bodies is variable. In some countries such as France and Germany, where the committees are chaired by the Ambassadors, these bodies have been effective (See France case study, Appendix I). But in others there is a much less successful record. Part of the problem is that they are not always attended by the relevant people in the different institutions, but the main reason is that their agendas are not strategic so they work as a forum to exchange information about forward plans and resolve possible areas of co-operation rather than trying to set a strategic agenda.

Co-ordination: the example of Team Norway

The name 'Team Norway' was adopted in the mid-90s to describe the close co-operation overseas between Embassies, the Norwegian Tourist Board, the Norwegian Export Council, the Norwegian Seafood Export Council, Chambers of Commerce and, in the US, the Norwegian Information Service. Originally a closely-integrated strategic approach, it now describes a looser cooperation and sharing of information, with each organisation working to its own targets but linking with the other organisations' activity where appropriate. In the US, Team Norway organisations on the East Coast meet every 7-8 weeks, with annual meetings for Team Norway organisations in the whole country. 'Team Norway' remains as a powerful slogan for member organisations.

Differentiation

British institutions are engaged in public diplomacy in almost every country in the world. Activities vary enormously between countries but this often has more to do with the personalities and history of the institutions based there than any strategic goals.

Why for example does the British Council organize excellent long-term political relationship building conferences in Italy (Pontignano) and Belgium (Anglo-Belgian Forum) but not in

France? Why does the FCO fund excellent scholarship programmes like the Atlantic and Greenwich fellowship in the United States, but not in European Union countries where strong links between policy-makers and media are equally important? Why is the BBC World Sevice funded to continue a Polish Service for a country that is developing rapidly and will shortly enter the European Union, at the same time as it is closing down its German and French Radio services? Will they close down the Polish Service when Poland enters the European Union? Why does the British Council host an impressive range of cultural activities in one developed country (France) and have merely a vestigial presence in another (the United States)?

What is needed is a clear strategy for these different types of countries with different goals for each of the institutions.

Within the most **developed** countries such as the other countries in the European Union, the United States and Japan, the UK should be aiming to strengthen the relationship as a partnership of equals. These countries, particularly European Union countries and the United States, are those which are of most importance for the UK, with strong shared political, economic and strategic interests, and there is huge untapped potential for the UK to learn from these countries. The aim should be for much greater mutual familiarity, with as much attention paid to turning around British perceptions of foreigners as to changing others' perceptions of Britain. Research shows that even in those countries with the closest contact with the UK, old-fashioned and unhelpful stereotypes persist in many people's minds, and the same is true in reverse. As well as greater familiarity, the UK should aim for genuinely mutually beneficial partnerships – creating channels for policy exchange and learning by building networks at all levels, from policy makers and journalists to school students and the voting public.

In **EU and Accession** countries particularly, the UK should be seeking in the first place to concentrate on the message that Britain is a committed and engaged member of the EU, and a very valuable present or future ally in the politics of the EU. Long-term political network and alliance building is the key to these bilateral relationships. In particular, the UK should aim to build and strengthen links between political parties within EU countries in order to create broad transnational political alliances that can both co-operate on issues at the European level and bring benefit to the countries individually through policy exchange. Additionally, as public opinion in different European countries is of such importance on many EU issues in which the UK has an interest, it should instigate proactive public diplomacy campaigns, targeted at important sections of foreign populations, in order to create some influence and leverage on these issues. Furthermore, in the current or future accession countries in Central and Eastern Europe, it is in the UK's interests to cultivate a stable and prosperous region, and to develop close ties with those countries which in the next few years will become fellow members of the European Union. The development of strong networks should be the main aim of public diplomacy in these areas.

In **developing countries** where the UK's interests are **competitive**, for example in emerging regional powers like South Africa and India (see case studies, Appendix I) the UK should act primarily with the aim of alleviating the negative association between globalisation and increased trading and investment linkages with these countries, and the spectre of a neo-colonialism. Several of the major transitional countries have ties to the UK largely as a result of a colonial legacy. This legacy may have left strong ties of language, history and institutions between the two countries, as well as long-term personal links through diaspora communities, but it will often also have resulted in ambivalent attitudes which need handling with sensitivity and awareness. One of the UK's main tasks in these countries therefore is to dispel the neo-colonial image by demonstrating good faith and mutuality of interest while engaging decision makers and influencers in global debates. One way of demonstrating the two-way nature of such relationships is by emphasising the UK's cultural pluralism and expanding schemes like the Visiting Arts programme to demonstrate that the West is receptive to influences from the developing world, and not merely an implacable exporter of a Coca-Cola culture and an exploitative economy. Other aims will be to harness positive links to strengthen economic ties and to encourage the development of partnerships in sectors such as technology.

Finally, in **developing countries** where the UK's interests are **co-operative**, it should adopt a strategy similar to that outlined above, namely one that downgrades the 'Britishness' of the UK's activities, and seeks to work in co-operation with the other Western countries whose interests in these areas are essentially indistinguishable from Britain's.

Evaluation

Where market research is about finding out about one's starting point, evaluation looks at the impact of activities. Unfortunately, it is very difficult to evaluate public diplomacy activity. While it is possible to measure changes in public opinion over time, there is no way of being certain what factor or combination of factors may have influenced this. In addition, while some facts may be easy to measure or quantify, these may not answer the most important questions. For example, an evaluation of press relations work based on the number of UK-related articles appearing in the media, or the number of column inches, fails to take into account the quality or content of the articles, or the negative articles which might have appeared if the press relations work had not happened. Nor do they measure what is ultimately of most importance, the articles' impact on readers, listeners or viewers.

- The solution adopted by the BBC World Service and the British Council is to use a combination of specific, measurable data and more general questions to gain as full a picture as possible. In many cases, the measurable data is used as a 'proxy' for the more important, but unmeasurable, impact of the activity.

- The BBC World Service carries out rolling annual surveys of numbers of listeners and continuous monitoring of on-line usage, and more detailed evaluation of attitudes towards its services in terms of both quality and trustworthiness in priority countries. In the past its main headline goal was number of listeners but this is being redefined to focus on a framework grouped around: reach (overall audience and target segments); reputation (trust); and impact (distinctiveness of the offer).

- The British Council has developed an evaluation methodology based on the 'Performance Scorecard' approach (currently in operation in 25 per cent of posts), where they track improved perceptions of the UK through follow-up surveys and story-boards. They will also monitor growth in the active membership of networks, virtual professional communities and alumni groups.

It is important that these different methods of evaluation are compatible with each other so that the FCO can get an overall sense of how the spectrum of institutions is working across the different dimensions of public diplomacy. This means that it is important to track outputs as well as outcomes – particularly as some of the outcomes will only materialise over the long-term. The US State Department has developed an impressive set of output indicators which are regularly monitored. They use sophisticated contact-management systems to track the amount of contact with each of the target groups (including face-to-face meetings, participation in seminars, attendance at film or cultural presentations, and use of the library, as well as follow-up contact). They gather data on the thematic breakdown of activities, formats, venues, and the range of partner organisations. Most impressively they track media coverage for each activity.

Multilateral Public Diplomacy: A Case Study

The paradox of diplomacy is that as it becomes more multilateral, it depends ever more on fluctuating national political debates. Achieving change on many foreign policy and the domestic issues will depend on forging international alliances and working through multilateral structures. But while the issues become more transnational, the pressure on governments will remain predominantly national - and sometimes even local.

Take CAP reform for example. The issues of concern in France are the support structures for French farmers, in Germany it is food safety and quality, while in Scandinavian countries the main arguments are about the environment and the impact on the developing world.

The challenge for public diplomacy is to link these competing national debates and map out a path for change. The goal will not just be to win the battle for public opinion at home - but to ensure that publics in a majority of countries see the issue from our perspective and exercise pressure for change on their national governments. Achieving these objectives demands a good deal of co-ordination between advocates of change - governmental and non-governmental.

The means reinventing bi-lateral relations so that they are focused on multilateral issues - and to use networking and events to link up different national debates and get third party validation for our ideas. The starting point should be a mobilisation of domestic departments. The Europe Minister, for example, could write a letter to all other departments saying inviting them to use public diplomacy to support their international policy needs - asking the domestic departments to list their priorities on particular issues and explain the barriers they have come up against. This can then lead to a concerted campaign across the three dimensions of public diplomacy:

a. News management

Launch a "step change" programme for the European media
It is important to deepen links with the foreign media in the capital and on the ground. In the same way that the British Government launched a 'step change' initiative which consisted of ministers and officials meeting their counterparts in all EU countries - a media initiative could encourage all ministers to do at least one interview with a journalist from each EU country on an issue of political importance.

Multilateralise responses
The key danger with multilateral issues - in each country - is for the media to paint a black and white picture of winners and losers which makes it difficult for each individual government to play their hands effectively. The key for each government will be to be able to show that they are in the mainstream, and have the material and information to multilateralise responses - in order to avoid being forced into defensive corners where they threaten to use the veto.

c. Pro-active Communications

Plan and co-ordinate activities and strategic messages with advocates of change.
Bring together all the key parties - both governmental and non-governmental to plan a strategic campaign and ensure that the public and media pressure reflects the right issues at the right times.

NGO Diplomacy
Work out which NGOs and interest groups have an interest in pursuing change and work with the NGOs in your country to build a multi-national alliance. This might be working with groups like the RSPB, Oxfam and the Consumers Association in Britain on CAP reform - and getting them to use their European umbrella groups to shape the debate in other countries.

d. Relationship building

Think-tank and political party diplomacy
The key solution is to get into a position where people from other countries come to issues from the same perspective as you - so that you do not need to persuade them. This is very difficult if their national, political, media and academic debates start from very different premises. For example, the debate on the future of the CAP in Brussels has traditionally been framed by the farming and agricultural policy community. Yet around the EU there are there are a series of disparate lobbies (development ngos, environmentalists, consumer groups, tax payers groups) who would benefit from reform, but because their perspectives have not been linked, it has been easy for the agenda to be set by farming ministries in hoc to their producer interests.

8. Conclusions and Recommendations

All governments pay lip-service to the way that the rise of global communications and the spread of democracy, the growth of global NGOs and the development of powerful multilateral organisations have changed the nature of power within societies, and altered the craft of government and diplomacy. But very few have adequately reflected it in the way that they deploy their resources, organise their activities, or go about their core business.

It is a paradox that, as interdependence has increased, the amount invested in nurturing relationships with the rest of the world has steadily declined. For some European countries this was a necessary adjustment to the end of empire, and the fact that many of the international engagements are conducted by domestic departments rather than through foreign ministries. But in Britain at least – in spite of the fact that cuts in the budgets of the FCO, British Council and BBC World Service have been reversed since 1997 – there is a continuing imbalance between the amount spent on (relatively cheap) preventive and proactive diplomacy and the (relatively expensive) military capabilities that we need to respond when things go wrong.

The biggest challenge is to the culture and priorities of foreign services themselves. Public diplomacy can no longer be seen as an add-on to the rest of diplomacy – it has to be seen as a central activity which is played out across many dimensions and with many partners. This will have serious implications for the way that resources are deployed. A substantial amount of the Foreign Office's budget is tied up in people and buildings – leaving very little to develop programmes which are capable of meeting our public diplomacy goals. Expenditure on buildings alone (running costs and capital expenditure) is £230 million, almost twice the British Council grant of £140 million. It is difficult to judge the exact amount of time spent on public diplomacy by individual diplomats, but only 5 per cent of FCO staff overseas are listed as coming under Objective 5 (broadly, Public Diplomacy) and 11 per cent in the UK. This is less than a quarter those engaged in consular services overseas (22 per cent).

There has also been a tendency to target public diplomacy resources on softer markets – rather than the most important developed countries - on the grounds that it is easier to have an impact there. This is putting the cart before the horse. If our analysis about the changing nature of power is correct, it follows that the key challenge is to develop a model of public diplomacy capable of having an impact in the countries that are of most strategic importance, and to deploy resources in a way which reflects those priorities.

Above all what is needed is a much broader and more creative idea of what public diplomacy is – and what it can do. The main overall conclusions of this report are:

- The government should **commit more resources** to public diplomacy which will become an increasingly important tool of influence on foreign and domestic policy. Public Diplomacy efforts should be **focused on the countries which are most important to our interests** rather than those which are perceived to be the easiest to influence.

- Additional expenditure of those resources should **concentrate on proactive messaging** and building **long-term political relationships**, and not on reactive, argumentative rebuttal.

News management needs to focus much more effectively on foreign correspondents based in London.

- Institutions need much **greater flexibility** (budgetary, physical, and in personnel terms) to be able to respond swiftly and effectively to short-term crises.

- The UK should differentiate its public diplomacy strategies in different countries, identifying where its interests are in **competitive** and where they are **co-operative**, and **prioritising bilateral expenditure** according to competitive importance.

- **There are potential savings** to be made in the **short term** by **stopping the production of news-feeds** by the FCO in London and instead concentrating on conducting research and producing resources on strategic messages which can be customised at post level. In the **medium term**, European Union funding should be sought to cover our activities in **co-operative countries** and we should explore the possibilities of merging the BBC's francophone Africa service with Radio France International to produce a co-operatively funded European service in Africa.

More detailed recommendations are grouped together below under the headings

- **Strategy and Co-ordination**

- **Differentiating Public Diplomacy on the Ground**

- **Covering the three dimensions** (News Management, Strategic Communication, Long-term Relationship Building)

- **Crisis Diplomacy**

- **Working Through Others**

- **Beyond Propaganda**

- **Professionalism and the Conduct of Public Diplomacy**

A. Strategy and Co-ordination

It is important to develop a way of planning for, and thinking about, the spectrum of public diplomacy activities in a strategic fashion.

In general, the Government should ensure that substantial resources in all the organisations are focused on the countries which are most important to our interests. This means ending the reluctance to spend resources on mature democracies - such as the US or France – where opinion is harder to change, but where British influence is critical to our foreign and domestic policy goals.

- The Foreign and Commonwealth Office, in consultation with the Ministry of Defence, Department for International Development, and domestic departments, should develop a clear strategy for Britain in the world. This can then act as a framework for the other organisations in their planning. The Public Diplomacy Strategy should contain:
    - a list of priority countries (including a sense of whether public diplomacy should be organised co-operatively or competitively);
    - one or two clear strategic messages;
    - target audiences;
    - a framework for explaining the roles of the different organisations;
    - a strategy for working with others beyond government.

- Co-ordination:
  - There must be a central body in London that has sufficient clout within all the public diplomacy organisations which is charged with ensuring strategic co-ordination – and making sure that there are no gaps in public diplomacy activities;
  - The Public Diplomacy Committees on the ground should be chaired by the Ambassador to ensure that they are reflected in all the activities of the mission;
  - The Public Diplomacy Committees' strategy should be built into each institution's strategic planning, so that, for example, British Council strategy should explicitly include overall public diplomacy strategy and public diplomacy work by other organisations as part of its working context.
  - All organisations should explore more effective ways of co-ordinating their activities with other EU Countries in both co-operative and competitive countries. One idea worth pursuing would be having a meeting of all the EU heads of mission in each country who could mandate the EU delegation to pursue shared goals in its public diplomacy activities.

B. Differentiating Public Diplomacy on the Ground

The Government should ensure that the public diplomacy it carries out in a given country is suitable for that country, rather than simply being a repetition of a 'one-size-fits-all' model of public diplomacy. In particular, there should be a decision about whether the nature of the national interest is competitive or whether it can be pursued co-operatively with other countries. The public diplomacy institutions should tailor the kind of public diplomacy they do, and the messages that they send, to those interests and conditions.

- The Foreign Office should create a target group of the 50 or so countries where it calculates that the UK has strong bilateral interests. All competitive aspects of public diplomacy in the remaining countries, including British 'branding' of governance programmes and attempts to promote our own interests at the expense of others should played down.
    - At the Copenhagen EU summit, the Government should propose a plan for European co-operation on activities of mutual interest, including promotion of democracy and human rights, democratic capacity-building, and the support of civil society and of media infrastructure, in non-competitive countries.
    - The British Council and BBC World Service should seek to deepen co-operation with similar European organisations. In particular the BBC should work with broadcasting services like RFI or Deutsche Welle, both in service provision and in media capacity building and training programmes in countries of co-operative rather than competitive interest.

Furthermore, the UK should differentiate its public diplomacy offering along the following lines:

- In all **developed** countries, there should be a large increase in public diplomacy resources. Public diplomacy work should concentrate on:
    - Campaigns of proactive communication aimed at media multipliers. Our core messages should be constantly promoted by the identification, promotion and placement of good news stories.
    - Long-term political relationship building, in the form of scholarship programmes like the Atlantic Fellowships, political party links and policy-exchange programmes.
    - Interest groups and NGOs, and particularly

campaigning NGOs, in order to disseminate messages to developed civil societies via their superior networks and credibility.

- A concerted push to market BBC World television as a platform for news to reflect the fact that television is by far the more important medium in developed countries, particularly for forming opinions about the UK. The Government should explore the prospect of channelling money into BBC World to make this possible.
- Co-operation with other countries, particularly EU countries, to promote the benefits of multilateral action to the world's developed nations.

• In **EU and Accession** countries, a particular subset of developed countries, the UK should:
  - Move to maximise our leverage in the EU's shared political space by providing money to develop powerful alliances between major political parties across the spectrum.
  - Actively target public diplomacy campaigns on key political issues, like CAP reform or asylum policy, to the key influential constituencies such as business, environmentalists and consumer groups in other countries.
  - Develop a programme of activities which stress the 'Europeaness' of Britain, to ensure we are considered to be central to EU politics and hence a vital ally for others.
  - Work with national think-tanks and political parties to develop an intergovernmental strand of thinking on the future of the European Union to counteract the more centralising agenda of the Brussels-based policy community.
  - Instigate a 'Step Change For Public Diplomacy' which mirrors the Step Change Programme by getting each

British Minister to give at least one interview a year to a major newspaper or TV programme in each member state.

- In **developing countries**, where the UK is pursuing **competitive interests**, for example India, we should concentrate on:
  - Targeting the 'successor generation' even more than is currently the case. In many of these key countries, Britain's influence is fading as the generation with which it has closest links passes away (see Case Studies, Appendix II).
  - Developing our capacity for using indigenous languages until all public diplomacy literature is available in more than one language.
  - Utilising Britain's diaspora communities to strengthen relations (see below.)
  - Emphasising cultural pluralism and mutuality of relations, for instance through an expansion of the Visiting Arts scheme (see below) in order to counteract the perception that, with increased openness to international marketplaces, Western culture is flooding out the indigenous cultures of these nations.
  - DFID should provide the Embassies in these countries with detailed information on the contribution of the UK to poverty reduction, citing specific newsworthy projects so that the Embassy's public affairs officers can utilise this very important source of positive impressions of the UK.

- In **developing** countries where the UK has **no significant bilateral interests**, public diplomacy should be carried out in a co-operative fashion with other developed countries, particularly other EU states:
  - There should be no 'great game' in public diplomacy,

where development assistance, international broadcasting, political assistance and exchanges are used to develop spheres of influence.

- There should be a push to create multilateral funds to carry out the large amount of very important public diplomacy activity in these countries. These should concentrate on conflict prevention, civil society capacity building, governance and political development and other areas.
- Greater investment should be poured into these co-operative funds.

C.   *Covering The Three Dimensions*

The government should develop a strategy for filling the gaps in the British public diplomacy effort.

- **News Management**
  It is important to bring structures for dealing with the media up to date to reflect the 24 hour news cycle and the increased importance of foreign correspondents in spreading the news:
  - All Whitehall departments should have liaison officers to communicate with the corps of foreign correspondents in London.
  - There should be much greater links between the Embassies and their respective London correspondents.
  - In the long term, there should be a move to develop a Government Information and Communication Service that covers both foreign and domestic policy. There should be much greater interplay with GICS, with secondments to all the bigger posts.
  - Embassy public affairs staff should be sufficiently senior for public diplomacy to have credibility as an equal 4th major strand of Embassy work alongside political,

consular and commercial.
- The Foreign Office should appoint a spokesperson of international stature to major media organizations like CNN and Al-Jazeera. It would help Britain's case if viewers got used to a regular speaker who could work to dispel stereotypes about Britain. For example, the US State Department brought back diplomat Christopher Ross from retirement to act as its public face in the Middle East.

- **Strategic Communication**
  British public diplomacy has not concentrated enough on the medium-term strategic delivery of key messages, but has instead focused too much on reactivity and rebuttal. We recommend that:
  - There should be proactive communications campaigns in all Embassies and British Council offices overseas, to spot and promote news stories that deliver these key messages.
  - To facilitate this, a central grid of all activities that can be made into news stories about Britain abroad should be produced and made available to overseas staff from a central base in London.
  - The institutions should make it their business to be aware of every UK-related event occurring in their country. No opportunity to present a positive story about the UK should be missed simply because an event is not on the initiative of one of the institutions. For example, Elton John concerts in Warsaw are excellent opportunities to emphasise the message that Britain is a creative country, even if he has not been invited by the British Council.
  - Activity in other countries should increasingly be 'UK' branded, not branded with the different institutional

logos (FCO, British Council, TPUK, etc.) – except in the rare circumstance where there is a clear case for giving priority to the institution rather than the UK as a whole. There should be a clear distinction of official government positions and events, but all other activity should be grouped under a single brand with a single logo.

• **Long-term relationship building**
There should be much more attention played to funding for long-term relationship development, as the most effective way of communicating positive messages about the UK and fostering good relations between the countries concerned. These kind of programmes have been successful in the fields of arts and education, but much more should be done outside these areas in politics, policy exchange and science.
  - The Chevening Scholarships and other exchange schemes like the Atlantic Fellowships, should be greatly increased in number and there should be much more concentration on converting those exchanges into long-term networks of relationships via follow up work.
  - In addition to boosting funding for the Chevenings, there should be a careful examination of their structure. Shorter time periods (e.g. a single term) could increase throughput and allow those high-flyers who cannot spare an entire year to participate. There should also be thought given to broadening the range of people who receive Chevenings – perhaps by reconsidering awarding them solely on a competitive basis and allocating some scholarships via nomination.
  - The British Council should be actively building lasting relationships with everyone that learns English by systematically profiling its client-base, building real and virtual networks.
  - The British Council should be actively building lasting

relationships with everyone that takes an examination through them by developing much clearer profiling and using the information to systematically target individuals.
- British Council websites should be used to build virtual networks, through policy discussion groups and arts discussion email lists.
- There shoud be a review of the branding, alumni schemes and follow up of all scholarships, teaching assistanceships and exchanges to ensure that they become as prestigious as the Fulbright, Rhodes scholarship and JET programme. In particular, we should examine whether the schemes should be renamed so that they make a positive statement about modern Britain.

D. Crisis Diplomacy

By understanding and planning for public diplomacy's central role in crises, it should be possible to develop responses to momentous events that reinforce rather than undermine our strategic message goals. The Government should:
- Ensure that there are pre-existing clear strategic messages. If these are well understood then it is easier to make sure that reactions to crises bolster them rather than detract from them.
- Build public diplomacy into crisis response teams at the beginning. If a broad coterie of the right partners are involved from the start, then the core crisis team will have a wide enough vision of how actions will impact internationally.
- Free up crisis response budgets by providing a centrally managed pot of money for crisis public diplomacy. This would then be flexible enough to provide

communications cover for unexpected eventualities.

- Ensure that there remains a residual staff ready to provide international co-ordination when the need arises. This could take the form of a skeleton Coalition Information Centre, keeping open lines of communication and capabilities that can be expanded at short notice.
- The FCO should set up a 'diplomatic SWAT team' capable of setting up a virtual embassy with public affairs potential within 24 hours anywhere in the world that a crisis could conceivably occur.

E. Beyond Propaganda

- Public diplomacy institutions should concentrate more on using our consumption of others' culture as a way of making pluralism a central part of the UK's public diplomacy message.
  - At least 10 per cent of British Council post budgets should be spent on bringing foreign artists, lecturers, journalists and politicians to the UK to perform or speak. The institutional implications of a greatly increased influx of sponsored visitors would have to be examined, and the question of whether to expand Visiting Arts or collapse its role into the British Council should be considered.
  - The scope of cultural imports should be much broader, with not just the arts but popular culture, politics, science, and academia catered for. The goal to be kept in mind should always be creating maximum impact in their countries of origin.
  - The UK should bring together the different schemes to recruit teaching assistants under a prestigious large-scale JET-style brand, where young foreign students are

funded to come and teach their languages in Britain for a
year, and a network of alumni should be created.

F. Working Through Others

In order to communicate with citizens who are sceptical of
'government information', the Government should make
working with non-governmental organisations an important
part of public diplomacy.

- On any issue where the Government has a message that is on
  the global agenda, it should seek out the key NGOs and ally
  with them – using their networks, skills, and credibility to
  attain mutual goals.
    - The FCO should have staff shadowing the most
      important NGOs, building relationships with them,
      helping them with problems that arise. This would build
      a secure foundation if close co-operation is required in
      the future.
    - It should be routine to share information with NGOs in
      areas of overlap, and to involve them in policy-planning
      where they have expertise.

- The UK should take further steps to use its many diaspora
  communities to advantage. These should include:
    - Instituting links to diaspora communities in the UK –
      diaspora diplomats – to strengthen relationships with
      their descendent country and to emphasise the UK's
      multicultural status.
    - Use members of the UK's diaspora communities as
      'ambassadors' to their origin country, to project positive
      messages about the UK as a tolerant and multi-ethnic
      culture.
    - The FCO, British Council, Invest UK, and TPUK should
      recruit heavily from diasporas, utilising pre-existing
      familiarity and language skills.

- The UK should concentrate on creating close relationships between domestic political parties and their counterparts in other countries. This should be an absolute priority in EU countries, where the shared political space makes it a pre-requisite for effectively seeing through European policies.
  - The British Council should be given an explicit authorization and additional resources to fund political party policy exchange and relationship building in exactly the same way as it does for think-tanks and other NGOs.
  - The British Council should be given the resources to develop its governance and civil society department so that it is capable of giving the same sort of programme support on long-term political relationship-building as it currently does on the arts.
  - The Government should examine the idea of giving funding to each of the main political parties in order to second programme officers to British Council Offices or Embassies in EU countries with a brief to improve relationships and mutual learning on policy issues between the United Kingdom's main parties and their European sister parties.

- The government should self-consciously try to associate itself with dynamic and modern British brands and try to get business to use its clout to build positive perceptions of Britain
  - The government should back a business-led programme for attracting talent to the UK from overseas by targeting the companies that have their European headquarters in London. This should include a series of aggressively marketed scholarships and placements. It could draw upon the British Council's education networks to identify and attract that talent.

G. Professionalism and the Conduct of Public Diplomacy

The conduct of public diplomacy by the UK's institutions should be reformed so as to incorporate professional communications skills. Areas that have an important effect on the overall impression of the UK, but that are currently neglected, should be actively tackled. Specifically:

- Translation budgets should be boosted to allow dissemination of all public diplomacy literature in the vernacular.
- All the public diplomacy institutions should be prepared to spend resources on buying in professional skills in marketing or design.
- It should be normal practice to conduct serious, large-scale research to understand our target audiences. We should identify gaps and target them, rather than attempting a blanket offering. One idea would be to team up with other countries to conduct benchmark surveys which would have greater credibility (the US spend roughly $5 million a year on polling).
- A less resource-intensive way of conducting market research is by online polling. This has been tried, for example, by the British Council in the first phase of their year 2000 market research survey of online services.

• Much greater attention should be paid to the experiential and gateway image aspects of the UK's national identity abroad. In particular:

- The premises of UK institutions abroad should suit the image of Britain which organisations are trying to convey.
- Visa processing should be used as an opportunity to convey positive messages about the UK through its

processes and premises. 100,000 people get visas in India every year, and they are very likely to be part of the growing middle class that the UK seeks to target. Visa application is consequently an important opportunity to present a positive image of Britain. Processes should be efficient and use modern technology; electronic visa applications should be made electronic rather than simply seen as an opportunity to cut out a third of the queuing. Premises should exemplify the best of British design through the layout, appearance and display material. Visa application should also be used as an opportunity to distribute literature about visiting the UK, places to stay, etc.

- Because the UK is an island, 80 per cent of its visitors come through five major gateways. This presents a unique opportunity to create a positive impression of the UK at the outset of any visit that is being comprehensively squandered by the anonymous, poorly lit, poorly designed public and retails spaces at these gateways. Because the airports are run by BAA, a private company, there are limits on what government can do to remedy this. But concerted political pressure should be put on the leadership of BAA to use its influence with the supply chain to radically improve the design and environment of these gateways.

- Additionally, the BTA should consider investing significant resources in presenting a modern, contemporary, creative image of Britain in these key spaces.

Appendix I: Public Diplomacy on the ground

A study of UK public diplomacy in the United States of America, France, Poland, India, South Africa, and the United Arab Emirates.

In considering the UK's relationships with other countries, it is clear that the very different relationships will give rise to different public diplomacy needs. In chapters Seven and Eight we set out a typology of countries and in this section how this is played out in practice in different types of countries. The following sections look at the UK's public diplomacy work in a number of example countries, and try to answer a series of questions.

The countries selected were:

- Two developed countries: the US and an EU member state, France

- One Central European transitional country: Poland

- Three developing countries with historical ties to the UK, all economically and politically important in their regions, including two with large Muslim populations: India, South Africa and the United Arab Emirates.

All six countries were selected for the strength of the public diplomacy work carried out there, to see what examples of good practice might be applicable elsewhere, and to examine what the effects of public diplomacy work can be.

Fact-finding visits to each country were necessarily short, and so the summaries below should not be taken as comprehensive, but as highlighting key points.

The questions we tried to cover are:

1. Do we commit enough resources to that country, given its importance in the world, and the kinds of relations we wish to foster with it?

2. Are we clear about what our strategic messages should be, and how successful have we been so far in putting those messages across?

3. Should we be seeking to act competitively or co-operatively with other countries in delivering our messages?

4. How successfully do we span the three dimensions of public diplomacy – from news management and rebuttal, through medium term strategic message delivery, to long-term relationship building? Also, how well do our institutions mesh together in covering that spectrum?

5. Are we seeking to develop relationships and foster trust with the right non-governmental partners in that country?

6. Are we targeting audiences and issues correctly, and utilizing the correct platforms for our messages?

7. Do we have the skill sets that we need in place to carry out public diplomacy on a professional basis?

8. Are our responses to crises in the relationship between the UK and the host country in line with our long-term goals?

The USA

The US-UK relationship: strengths

Strong historical and cultural links and a common language

Close foreign policy and security relationship
Military cooperation in Kosovo, the Gulf, Bosnia and Afghanistan

Shared membership of key multilateral organisations, especially the UN Security Council and NATO

Close commercial links
- Both countries are the largest overseas investor in each other's economy
- UK exports to the US total £30 billion
- The twin importance of New York and London as the world's leading financial centres

Personal contact
- Personal and family ties
- 4 million US visitors to the UK each year
- 40,000 US students currently in the UK

Shared cultural space
- Shared cultural history
- US film and music in the UK
- Interest in British film and music among the under-25 age group in the US

Strong academic and scientific links
- 10 per cent of professors in the Harvard Faculty of Sciences are British

Close ties between the media in both countries, including exchange of personnel

Strengthening of the US-UK relationship after the September 11th attacks
- US public appreciation of the UK's support after September 11th
- Strong personal relationship between President Bush and Tony Blair since September 11th

The US-UK relationship: weaknesses

US attitudes towards the UK tend to be stereotyped and out of date
- Survey data shows many Americans consider the British to be conservative, old-fashioned, arrogant, and not technologically advanced

Demographic and social changes mean that groups who do not share traditional links with the UK are increasingly influential

The US is commercially self-sufficient and has no real need for British products
- No competitive advantage in most sectors in being recognised as British
- Many British firms brand themselves as American or Canadian for the American market

Irish-American support for the Republican movement in Northern Ireland
- A vocal pro-Republican Irish-American lobby, particularly in Boston and New York, sees Britain as the enemy
- Some media, such as the Boston Globe, print anti-British stories about Northern Ireland
- Sinn Fein and the IRA receive much of their funding from pro-Republican Americans

Trade disputes between the US and the EU

Some disagreements on global policy issues such as Kyoto

Foot & Mouth Disease and the race riots in the north of England in the summer of 2001 received a lot of negative media coverage and discouraged many people from visiting Britain

UK public diplomacy in the US

Strengths

Substantial resources are put into what is the largest programme of UK public diplomacy activity worldwide, with a network of offices in thirteen major cities managing public diplomacy activities

Tony Blair's 'Shoulder to Shoulder' speech, the playing of The Star Spangled Banner at Buckingham Palace, and Blair's visit to Washington shortly after September 11th very well received

British Film Office in Los Angeles which promotes the UK film industry in the US

The BBC has a good reputation for the quality of its international news

Atlantic fellowships excellent model for public diplomacy

Weaknesses

The British Council is disproportion-ately small

BBC programmes shown on Public Service Television tend to perpetuate a stereotyped view of the UK

Impact of the BBC is still low among general public, although they claim to reach 24 per cent of cosmopolitans in key cities on the East Coast

Opportunities

TV is the main medium for news, information and entertainment

Appetite for global news post September 11th.

The highly developed electronic communications environment leads to high expectations

Increased demand for international education

Threats

The size and diversity of the US presents a challenge

Demographic changes in the US

The radio market is very segmented, with about 10,000 radio stations. Public service radio only attracts 5-6 per cent of the adult radio audience

Competition for those wishing to study overseas both from other Anglophone countries and from other EU countries

Interest among policy-makers in international good practice, and many shared policy issues	Reduction in number of students studying British politics over the last 25 years
Large number of alumni: over 1,300 Marshall scholarships to date	

The US is, as is widely recognised, the most important and influential country in the world: its first and only hyperpower. The UK's relationship with the US is remarkably strong, one might even say special, and is a product of powerful historical, linguistic and cultural links. As a result, 'the market' takes care of a great deal of the relationship very well. Commercial ties are powerful, with deep interpenetration of investment capital, and strong links between New York and London as two of the World's financial capitals. Interpersonal contact is equally high, with 4 million visitors a year from the US coming to Britain on top of the 40,000 students studying here. When the strength of these 'market' links is coupled with the difficulty of producing public diplomacy impact within such a sophisticated society with a plethora of different media outlets, the conclusion might be drawn that public diplomacy in the US can largely be left to its own devices.

Yet given the USA's unusually disproportionate importance, and the existence of real market failures in its relationship with the UK on some issues, notably areas of difference in broad political stance, we should be all the more clear-eyed about what specific areas of the relationship need addressing, and all the more committed in dealing with them.

The two chief messages that the British Embassy seeks to put across about the UK are firstly that we are the closest and most natural ally of the US, and secondly that we are an innovative and modern country. Efforts on the first score have been, on any measure, fantastically successful. British actions after September 11th have been by far the single biggest influence in reinforcing a perception that was already very widely held. Blair's 'Shoulder to shoulder' speech, and the playing of the Star-Spangled Banner at Buckingham Palace, followed by Blair's visit to Washington shortly after the attacks, have undoubtedly impacted very positively on popular perceptions of the UK amongst the US public. Another example of responsive and effective public diplomacy in this area was the UKwithNY festival held in October 2001. Although planned before the September 11th attacks, this event was carefully adapted to put across a strong message of UK-US solidarity at a difficult time – a message that seems to have been very effectively communicated. There is also evidence that the UK is peculiarly differentiated from other European countries in this area, a result in part, no doubt, due to Tony Blair's stance on US policy that contrasted with the critical statements of many European politicians, and of EU Foreign Affairs Commissioner Chris Patten.

On the second score – presenting Britain as an innovative, creative and exciting country – efforts have been less successful, partly because they have had to work against public pre-conceptions rather than with them. Surveys of attitudes in the US towards Britain have revealed that the common stereotype is of a country that is technologically backward, old-fashioned and conservative, and even somewhat arrogant. The British Council's work in presenting a diverse and contemporary selection of British arts – including events like the Great Expectations exhibition of innovative British design – and also the scheduling on BBC America of programmes that challenge the more traditional stereotypes of the UK popular on American television go some way to addressing this weakness in the UK's image. Similarly, British Council targeting of publishers in the promotion of British writers, the British Film Office's promotion of the UK film industry through its office in Los Angeles, and the ongoing work the British Council does in providing information to US arts events funders and building links between them and UK artists, is intended to alleviate this problem. But progress towards this second overarching public diplomacy aim suffers in comparison with the success of efforts to promote the first.

One gap in strategic message presentation that is not fully addressed by British public diplomacy work in the US is around the issue of multilateralism. The general European enthusiasm for transferring national sovereignty to multilateral institutions like the EU, or for multilateral agreements like the Kyoto treaty on climate change, can be regarded with surprise amongst policy-making circles in the US. This is an issue of cognitive dissonance, where the case for multilateralism which Europeans have found convincing has not been effectively made to the Americans in such a way that they can at least recognise the basis for European enthusiasm. This presentation work – similar in kind to the political presentation work being done in the UK to 'sell' Europe – is perhaps not something that the Embassy would wish to be involved directly in, but it is an area where the British Council might usefully be more active.

It is important to note at this point that although the UK's crisis response public diplomacy in the US has been highly successful (as detailed above) it has somewhat neglected this multilateral strand of the UK's strategic messages to the US. There is a tension between emphasising the UK as the US's closest and natural ally (the concentration of most public diplomacy work after September 11th) and trying to highlight the arguments for multilateralism. In concentrating on the first, the UK has perhaps lost sight of the second. The ramifications of this have significance for more than just US-UK relations, as will be brought out more clearly in the French case study, below.

Presentation of the case for multilateralism is also a message where co-operation with other European partners would be mutually beneficial. In general terms, the UK has a considerable advantage in carrying out its public diplomacy in the US bilaterally, but in this case the deficiencies of EU and other countries' relationships with the US impact detrimentally on the UK, and so we should work closely with other European countries to improve the image of multilateral activity and institutions with the US policy elite. One way of achieving this beneficial co-operation would be for the various Ambassadors of the EU countries to jointly mandate the EU delegation in Washington to actively promote a European position on multilateral co-operation to the US.

In terms of trust-building work with the right groups, British public diplomacy is well-placed, and building on a good foundation. Overall British foreign policy, and the historic links between the two countries particularly in the two world wars, affords us a distinct comparative advantage in this area. Consequently, much work has been well-directed at key or problem areas. One example of both of these targets being hit at once is the Consulate in Boston. This not only works well in developing links with the influential Harvard and MIT academic communities, but is very active in dealing with the difficulties arising from the strong Irish Republican links in the city. For example, the consulate undertakes important media work in briefing the Boston Globe on stories that reflect well on the UK to counteract its long-standing inclination to take up a pro-Republican, anti-British stance on the issue of Northern Ireland

UK public diplomacy work in the USA spans the three dimensions of public diplomacy well. Short-term news management and rebuttal activity is carried out effectively by the embassy, and the work done in fostering long-term relationship-building should be singled out for praise as an example of good practice. Here the UK builds on a firm base of elite links. Educational ties are very close, with the success of long-running scholarship exchanges like the Fulbright and Marshall Scholarships perhaps reflected in the fact that 10 per cent of professors in Harvard's Faculty of Arts and Sciences are of UK origin. On top of this baseline of familiarity, programmes like the Atlantic Fellowships are excellent ways to promote policy and idea exchange. In this ongoing programme, pre-eminent experts in a variety of policy fields are invited take up 3 month fellowships in the UK, thus simultaneously re-invigorating the UK's policy debate and fostering high-level links into the American political establishment. (The importance of these academic and policy-making ties should not be underestimated, particularly in a country like America where a 'revolving door' operates between the large academic institutions and foundations like the Rockefeller and influential positions in government.) Similarly excellent relationship building work also goes on in the fields of media and finance, with the Greenwich and City fellowships respectively.

Two suggestions for improvement of the delivery of public diplomacy in the US might, however, be ventured. The first is the relative weakness of medium term message delivery, particularly when considered in comparison to the strength of the short and long-term public diplomacy work. The embassy could do more in organising an ongoing series of stories to be placed in the US media over the year to put across some of the UK's strategic messages to the US, like the case for multilateralism. The second area for improvement is the co-ordination and location of the two major UK public diplomacy institutions, the Embassy and the British Council. The relationship between the Embassy and the British Council has been bad in the past, and good co-operation between those two institutions is of course key to an effective overall strategy.

Furthermore, the choice of location for the offices of certain bodies is questionable. Placing the British Council Office (which is proportionately small compared to the size and importance of the USA as a target market) in Washington rather than in New York hampers its work by placing it at a remove from the cultural capital of the East Coast. The British Film Office's location in Los Angeles is a well thought out decision, but its lonely position as a British cultural diplomacy institution on the West Coast highlights the East Coast-centred nature of British public diplomacy in the US. There is a case for suggesting that by concentrating on the Eastern Seaboard cities, and particularly on Washington, we are in effect preaching to the converted, the most Anglo-centric and cosmopolitan US citizens, and that the UK would do much better to concentrate on the major cultural centres of the West Coast like LA and Seattle.

It is to the credit of the Embassy and the British Council in Washington that the full extent of this danger – that the UK be left communicating with its 'natural constituency' on the Eastern Seaboard whilst the demographic balance in the USA shifts decisively to the West and South – has been recognised. It is, in fact, a major preoccupation of the Embassy from the Ambassador downwards, and with good reason as the results from the 2000 US census demonstrate. The US, alone among industrialised nations, continues to grow rapidly in population terms – overwhelmingly as a result of immigration from Latin America and Asia to the Western and Southern States of the US. The Hispanic and Asian populations grew by 58 per cent and 37 per cent respectively from 1990 to 2000, and Whites are now a minority in 48 of the largest 100 cities in the US, up from 30 in 1990.

The conscious effort to broaden the makeup of the various Fellowship schemes – Atlantic, City and Greenwich – is one example of a positive step in this direction. But it is vital to realise that these demographic swings in terms of ethnic composition of the population and in geographical distribution (States in the South and West grew twice as fast as those in the North and Midwest in the 1990s, and now contain almost 60 per cent of Americans) require a paradigm shift in the conduct of public diplomacy in the USA, and not simply tinkering or re-orientation of existing schemes and methods. In a country where George W. Bush finds significant advantage in his ability to deliver campaign speeches in Spanish, it is vital that UK public diplomacy be conducted in that language as well. Equally, in a country where 12 per cent of the population is black, conscious exposure of the UK's own large black population ought to be central to our public diplomacy strategy.

Finally, there are areas and opportunities that the UK is failing to effectively utilize. One example of this is the large contingent US press corps based in London. These correspondents represent a key constituency for UK public diplomacy, with great influence and the capacity to disseminate stories to a great number of people. They should be integrated fully in any UK public diplomacy strategy for the USA, but at present are underused in communicating with the American public.

A second opportunity that is being missed is in the area of television news. The BBC puts across a diverse image of Britain well to a large number of people. The World Service has been effective in getting its programs carried on over 100 US stations, including Public Radio in all of America's top 20 cities, and can now claim 24 per cent of its chief target audience ('cosmopolitans' in Boston, New York and Washington) tuning in every week. However, the USA (along with most of the developed world) receives the overwhelming majority of its news not by radio but by television. The most effective way to communicate British objectivity and high standards of independent analysis in its news service to a significant number of Americans is to concentrate resource on marketing BBC World as the BBC news platform in the US – a move that requires significantly increased resources being allocated.

Norwegian Public Diplomacy in the US

Norway's image in the US

The prevailing image of Norway in the US stems from Norwegian immigrants, who have settled particularly in the mid-West but also in New York, Chicago and Seattle. The image is on balance positive, (in contrast to, say, German immigrants from the 1930s, whose image of Germany is considerably more negative) but could not really be considered reflective of contemporary Norway.

The Norwegian Information Service wants to balance this with a contemporary image of an internationally active country concerned with human rights, along the lines of the Canadian or other Scandinavian image, but doesn't wish to replace the old image entirely.

Other positive associations come from its history in WWII, and membership of NATO. The only major negative association stems from commitment to whaling.

The Norwegian Information Services in New York covers the whole of US and is based in New York as 'world capital of culture and economics' (compare the British Council's location in Washington). It is also moving from print-based to web-based information material.

Norway seeks to focus on school children and universities with Scandinavian departments. It provides schools with a study unit, 'Learning about Norway', designed for teachers and children. This is distributed to 15-20,000 teachers in print & electronically.

Norway recognises that just being reactive in its media management will not work because there are few opportunities in the normal course of events for Norwegian stories. Instead it seeks to create its own events which will generate media attention and concentrates resources on these - for instance the annual Norwegian Run in Central Park, with up to 5,000 people attending, or the annual Norwegian Christmas tree illumination at Union Station in Washington.

It also runs a major visitors programme in Washington which gets future members of Congress to visit Norway. Washington puts reciprocal emphasis on getting visitors to Norway.

France

The French-British relationship: strengths

High level of personal contact and familiarity
- 12 million British people visit France each year, and over 3 million French visit the UK.
- Over 100,000 visit the UK from France each year to learn English.
- Over 12,000 French students are currently studying at UK universities.
- 1,800 UK firms in France, and over 1,500 French firms in the UK.
- 955 town twinnings

Geographical closeness and good communication links:
- The Paris-London air route is the busiest in the world, carrying 3.3 million passengers each year.
- Eurostar and Eurotunnel

Large number of French correspondents in London

Rapidly increasing internet use
- 2.8 million people had internet access in 1999, a figure which has continued to rise since then.

Interest in British arts
- 400,000 people attended a British Council exhibition on Bacon in 1996.
- London a popular destination for young people, particularly for its nightlife and 'ethnic' music.

Extensive commercial links
- France is the UK's 3rd largest export market and 3rd largest supplier after the US and Germany; the UK is France's 3rd largest export supplier.

The French-British relationship: weaknesses

Traditional suspicion between the two countries

UK not in the Euro

Agricultural crises: BSE and FMD
- Boycott of French goods in UK supermarkets

Problems with the UK health service and transport system

Suspicion of UK liberal economics and closeness to the US

Perception of UK as anti-EU

Relatively poor knowledge of each others' languages

Strengths	Weaknesses
Web-based information in French on Embassy and British Council websites	No BBC World Service presence on FM due to high costs of FM frequencies
Good links with French journalists based in the UK	BBC Online in French is targeted not at France but at Francophone Africa
Commercial and cultural activities outside the capital	Foreign Office publications in English are of limited use in France
Seminars on policy issues	Journalists' visits not targeted at those already in the UK
Redesigned public space at the British Council offering videoconferencing and electronic information resources	
Regular high-profile events featuring British design, visual and performing arts	
English teaching for young learners, with British teachers and authentic materials	
Scholarships and exchanges, especially two-way programmes	
Campaign by Embassy and BTA in response to BSE and FMD	
Opportunities	**Threats**
High value placed on culture	Reduction in British Council funding
Influential national press and strong regional press	Reduction in the Chevening scholarship programme
No UK-style tabloid press	
Anniversary of Entente Cordiale in 2004	
UK excellence in scientific fields including IT and biotechnology	
Annual midsummer 'Fete de la Musique'	
Rapidly increasing internet use	

France is a critical target for UK public diplomacy not solely because it is in the EU, but because it is one of the EU's pivotal members. On many of the key issues where Britain is intensively seeking leverage and support from other EU countries, France is the most important country we need to win over. It is France that we must persuade to secure reform of the CAP – a political problem we have been attempting to deal with for decades. It is also France which is obstructing the opening of its energy markets, a major obstacle in the continuing process of European economic reform. As such, France must be one of our highest resources priorities for public diplomacy. But on the contrary, the UK appears to be making a serious mistake in cutting back funding for public diplomacy in France in general, including reducing the number of Chevening scholarships, and squeezing the British Council budget. This trend could well be damaging in the long term.

Some justification for these cuts might be offered by pointing to the thickness of informal and market relationships between the UK and France. France is the UK's third largest trading partner after the US and Germany, and is host to over 1800 UK firms. Stimulated by Eurostar's convenience, the large number of tourist visits between the two countries (12 million from the UK to France, 3 million back the other way) make for a high level of superficial familiarity. Furthermore, the UK receives over 100,000 visits a year from French seeking to learn English. But this unquestionably high level of commercial and personal linkage is not putting across the sophisticated political messages that are required to maximise the impact of public diplomacy in a shared political space like the EU.

The key strategic message which the UK is seeking to put across in France is that it is, in fact, a European country. There are two strands to the French suspicion that this message seeks to respond too. In the first place is the suspicion that the British do not share the same values as continental Europeans: values of social justice and welfare capitalism, rather than doctrinaire market liberalism. Linked to this is the suspicion that the UK is at best a half-hearted European country, which keeps more than half an eye across the Atlantic, and where Blair can be caricatured as George Bush's poodle. These suspicions are based in part on old antagonism, and on a history of post-war European relations where De Gaulle's 'Non' and Margaret Thatcher's echoing negative some years later seemed to set the tone for British-European relations. Contemporary evidence of this is identified in the UK's reluctance to join the Euro, and in New Labour's 'Third Way' which was regarded in some circles across the channel as some kind of smokescreen for an essentially free-market liberal economics.

UK efforts to demonstrate its closeness to the US unfortunately meant that the pro-European message became lost in the rhetoric of standing shoulder to shoulder with friends across the Atlantic.

The British Beef scandal highlighted the final important strategic message that the UK seeks to put across in France, which is to emphasise the quality and trustworthiness of British science. This is a readily identifiable weakness in the French image of the UK. 15 per cent of French professionals interviewed in the British Council's 'Through Other Eyes' survey were mainly or very unfavourable to the statement that the UK has a strong reputation for science – only China and Turkey though less of British science than the French. There are important efforts being made on this score, building on the work done in the short term during the Beef crisis. These focus on facilitating and highlighting areas of scientific co-operation through things like the Alliance Partnership, or the Prix Franco-Brittanique awarded to young French and British scientists.

In terms of effective trust-building, UK public diplomacy in France suffers from an initial disadvantage in that both populations have relatively poor knowledge of each other's languages, which obviously leads to difficulties in communicating with the wider French public. The institutions in France are well aware of this problem, and are taking important positive steps to remedy it. In particular, the growing use of the internet in France (2.8 million with access in 1999 – a figure that continues to rise) has allowed for easy presentation of documents and material in both French and English. Both the Embassy and the British Council websites are available in both French and English, and hits on the British Council website have in fact increased by a factor of 80 following that language provision.

However, the BBC's presence in France is minimal, and there is no French language TV service in what is predominantly a television-based market. BBC World Service is not available on FM in France due to the high cost of FM frequencies in developed markets, and in any case the World Service's French language service is primarily targeted at Francophone Africa. Providing sufficient investment to boost BBC TV in France, as the more popular medium, and to provide high-quality programming that would appeal to a French audience, in French, is probably an unrealistic suggestion. Nevertheless, there could usefully be a strategy for targeting French broadcast media to increase exposure of British programming.

Additionally, there should be more concentration on long-term language training, especially through residential exchanges. The Japanese have pioneered an excellent and very large scale scheme to invite young people over on JET schemes to teach

English for a year in Japan – a scheme that is then capitalised on with a great deal of follow-up, network building, and long-term relationship development. The range of teaching assistanceships that are organized by the British Council do not have the same prestige and profile as the Japanese scheme. There is a strong case in bringing the various schemes together under a stronger brand, similar to the JET scheme, which would improve British language skills in French, and create a caucus of young French with greater experience of both English and of the UK.

One consideration that requires more attention in UK public diplomacy in France is the need to reach the right constituencies with the UK's key messages. The groups that it is important for us to reach, particularly in connection with our high priority political issues like CAP reform and liberalisation of energy markets, lay primarily outside of the Metropolitan audience at which the majority of UK work is directed (and who are most likely to have direct experience and personal links with the UK). The UK needs to work with farmers and consumer groups in order to directly tackle its priorities in France. Some excellent work has already been done in this regard – particularly the visits made by British vets during the BSE crisis – but more could be done in reaching these audiences. In this regard the strength of the French regional press, certainly in comparison with the centralised media of the UK, could well be an asset and is an important target for more intensive media liaison work.

In terms of co-ordination between the various UK public diplomacy institutions in France, and of coverage of the whole spectrum of public diplomacy from short to long term, the picture in France is generally positive. The institutions work well together and their public diplomacy strategic planning is amongst the best in any country and could serve as a model for other countries. The closeness of this relationship is in part a result of the peculiar pervasiveness of the French state, which leads the British Council to work through the Embassy on most issues as formal relations with the French state will commonly form part of any large scale project.

As mentioned above, short-term crisis response and media rebuttal in France is conducted well and professionally. The weaknesses in coverage come at the long-term end of the spectrum. The majority of longer-term co-ordinated public diplomacy campaigns focus on the creative/innovative image of the UK, and consist largely of arts events (often highly successful ones: over 400,000 people attended a British Council Bacon exhibition in the mid 1990s).

There has, however, been a neglect of the political issues that are a vital point of UK-French relations. There should be a sustained campaign to work up good news stories around, say, CAP reform or British commitment to Europe. One under-utilised resource in this regard is the significant cohort of French press in London. These should be targeted by the Foreign Office in Whitehall, and by the other government departments, on a systematic basis and in co-operation with the Embassy in Paris – briefing in French and providing French translations of ministerial speeches. These British news could then be an excellent source of pro-British stories in the French press, and a good conduit for political messages that the UK seeks to deliver to the French public.

More serious is the weakness in long-term relationships, particularly in the policy arena. While there are around 12,000 French students studying at UK universities, these kind of links are not being systematically followed up to create networks of French people with extensive experience of the UK and of English. Furthermore, the scaling down of the Chevening scholarship programme – the Foreign Office's programme of scholarships targeted at future decision-makers – to only seven Chevening awards in 2001/2 is very unfortunate in this regard. The programme is an excellent way of ensuring that some of the top people in politics, business and the media have the kind of understanding of Britain that can only be gained by spending time in the country. Given the importance of France to the UK within the EU, additional investment in the scholarship programme now would undoubtedly pay dividends in the future.

This criticism leads on to a wider gap in Franco-British relations and in British public diplomacy in France. In the context of French and British sovereignty-sharing in the EU, and of the importance of demonstrating the UK's fundamentally shared political values with the continent, it is strange to that there is no scheme that corresponds to the Atlantic Fellowships scheme in the USA. The potential for future policy co-operation and for cross-fertilisation of policy ideas within the EU context that such a scheme would offer is significant. Furthermore, the British Council is not resourced to help in fostering links between French and English political parties, and whilst it is prepared to hold some political seminars it is not able to undertake this on a more systematic basis. It is vital for an effective UK political presence on the European stage that we forge alliances with continental political parties, and engage in debate and policy exchange with continental think-tanks and other institutions. Work that follows the lines of the German Stiftungen in other sophisticated and integrated European polities like France would be an important public diplomacy asset, and is conspicuously lacking in public diplomacy efforts at present.

Poland

The Poland-UK relationship: strengths

The two governments have excellent bilateral relations

The Polish and UK governments share a similar non-federalist, pro-enlargement attitude towards the EU

Poland is the UK's largest trading partner in Central and Eastern Europe

Historical links, especially cooperation during the Second World War, have left a mutually positive relationship, particularly among the older generation

Poles are relatively well-informed about the UK: in a 1999 public opinion survey, 60 per cent of educated young Poles claimed to know at least 'a fair amount' about the UK

In the same survey, 74 per cent of young educated Poles said they felt 'very' or 'mainly favourable' towards the UK - higher than either the US or Germany

British democracy and the legal system are rated highly in Poland, and Britain is thought of as multicultural and racially tolerant

In the same survey, 84 per cent of respondents perceived British goods and services as very or fairly good, and only 1 per cent as poor

83 per cent think British higher education is either fairly or very good. British media are rated highly in terms of both quality and trustworthiness

Polish businesses are keen to work with British companies, and would like to see more British companies in Poland

Sizeable Polish diaspora in the UK which is generally well regarded in both countries

English is widely spoken: 91 per cent of young educated Poles speak English, and the remaining 9 per cent wish to learn

39 per cent of educated young Poles have visited the UK at least once

> ## The Poland-UK relationship: weaknesses
>
> Images of the UK tend to be stereotyped and traditional
>
> Many Poles feel that Britain does not value its relationship with the EU
>
> The UK is not able to compete with the strength of Germany's influence as Poland's strongest ally in the EU
>
> UK investment in Poland ranks only sixth, behind that of Germany, the USA, France, the Netherlands and Italy, and many British companies are not widely recognised as being British
>
> In the survey quoted above, 69 per cent of respondents agreed with the proposition that the UK is not very welcoming towards foreigners
>
> Focus group discussions with young educated Poles in 1999 showed that British businessmen are regarded as being unwilling to take risks and to compete successfully in a competitive environment
>
> Knowledge of Poland in the UK is very limited
>
> Legacy of resentment of the UK's role during the Second World War, and the feeling it let Poland down
>
> Bad publicity associated with incidents of Poles being refused entry to the UK at UK airports

As the largest of the EU accession countries with a population of 40 million, Poland will be an important new voice within the shared political space of the EU. Poland will wield the same number of votes in the Commission as Spain, and only two less than the 'Big Four' – the UK, Germany, France and Italy. In spite of Germany's huge influence in Poland, with its strong commercial and cultural ties, in EU policy terms the Polish government is closer to the UK's position than to the federalist vision of Germany, making the UK and Poland natural allies. It is, therefore, very much in the UK's interest to be seen as interested in and engaged with Poland, to build networks between the respective political leaders and to foster mutual sympathy and understanding between the two populations. Given that other EU member states such as Germany and France have similar interests, the UK must also try to offer something distinctive.

UK public diplomacy in Poland

Strengths	Weaknesses
British Council highly regarded for its role during Communism	Embassy premises do not present modern front
BBC World Service Polish service is widely recognised and respected for its quality and trustworthiness, and judged the highest-quality news provider in Poland	Strategic planning between different agencies is weak
DFID's 'Know How Fund' is widely recognised	

Opportunities	Threats
Largest EU accession country with a population of nearly 40 million	Future Eastern border of the EU, with eastern neighbours a possible threat to stability
Expected to join the EU in 2004	Reducing importance of radio as a source of information and entertainment
One of the fastest growing economies in Europe, with annual growth of 3.8 per cent	Weaknesses in border management, environment and corruption need resolving prior to EU accession
NATO member	
Poland keen to form a bridge between the EU and Ukraine	Need to restructure the agricultural sector

Stemming from this accepted importance, the UK commits significant resources to public diplomacy in Poland (and in the other EU accession countries). In fact, Poland stands as a good model of a country where public diplomacy has been taken very seriously indeed. Nevertheless, the UK public diplomacy effort in the UK is being out-spent by German public diplomacy, which, for historical and geographical reasons, places a very high priority on good relations with the Poles.

The UK's strategic messages in Poland are determined to a large extent by the nature of our chief bilateral interest there, EU relations, and also by the baseline of Polish public opinion toward the UK, as revealed in the British Council's 'Through Other Eyes' survey of young educated professionals in a series of countries. That survey revealed relatively high levels of Polish familiarity with and favourability toward the UK. 60 per cent of those surveyed claimed to know 'a fair amount' about the UK, and 74 per cent felt 'very' or 'mainly' favourable – a figure that exceeded both American and German scores. However, despite warm Polish opinions toward the UK, they did not perceive it as a committed European country. Lack of interest in the EU was perceived as the UK's major weakness by 13 per cent of Poles – second only to its conservatism and lack of innovation at 14 per cent. Almost a quarter felt that the UK cared 'not a lot/not at all' for its relations with the EU (a sense of rejection echoed by the French and the Germans surveyed). Stemming from this baseline, it is therefore important for the UK to project itself as a key partner and a serious player in the EU. If alliance on EU issues is one of the chief advantages we wish to gain from our relations with Poland, then we cannot afford to appear as if the EU is not a top priority for the UK; because if that does seem to be the case then we will not appear attractive allies for the Poles.

The second chief consideration for the strategic public diplomacy relationship with Poland is that, as well as appearing less committed to Europe than other EU countries, we are also regarded as less important to Polish national interests than Germany. In the 'Through Other Eyes' survey, Germany was associated more strongly than the UK with innovation and 'world-beating companies', and was regarded by a higher proportion of people as a major financial and trading centre. The clear overall impression of Poles was that Germany was the economic powerhouse of the EU, and consequently the chief source of the investment and jobs that would stem from EU membership. This impression is also backed up by the figures, which have the UK ranking only sixth for inward investment in Poland, behind Germany, the USA, France, the Netherlands and Italy. This means there is a need for a strong commercial public diplomacy message, to convince Poland of the strength of British business. It also means that the British relationship with Poland is at a disadvantage, particularly relative to the German-Polish relationship, in being seen to be able to back its warm words and promises with concrete advantages to Poland.

The two key messages, therefore, that the UK seeks to convey in Poland are firstly that we are committed Europeans, and second that we are a country with serious economic and political weight on the European scene. Both of these messages combine to present the UK as a key political ally in European politics once Poland has successfully acceded to the EU.

UK public diplomacy in Poland has been in the main very successful at delivering these messages, particularly through the medium and long-term aspects of the relationship. Notable in this regard have been the UK's high-profile development work, the World Service's broadcasting, and the British Council's scholarship programmes.

The British Government, through the Embassy, has made considerable contributions to Poland's development during the post-Communist decade of transition. The Department for International Development's 'Know How Fund' (which is administered through the Embassy) has disbursed over £100m on development projects in support of Poland's development as a market economy since 1989. This work has been widely recognised, and is an excellent way of demonstrating the UK's commitment to the economic strength of Poland and the wider

EU. Furthermore, in 1999 an FCO-funded Action Plan, worth around £125,000 was launched to help Poland prepare for the technical aspects of EU membership in areas like Trade, Justice and Home Affairs, Agriculture and the Environment. The British have also contributed to readying Poland's armed forces for NATO accession through the ASSIST programme, of military and English language training. Development work of this kind, particularly when it gains a high local profile like DFID's 'Know How Fund' work has, makes a very positive long-term impact on UK-Polish relations.

The British Council's wealth of scholarship programmes in Poland are another effective way of influencing the long-term relations of the two countries, by exposing Poland's future decision-makers to the UK at an early stage. In addition to the 15 Joseph Conrad scholarships – the locally branded version of the FCO's Chevening scholarships – the British Council also provides funding for young lawyers, scientists and businesspeople through individual schemes. In fact the British Council's reputation in Poland generally is very good, stemming at least in part from positive associations with its work in Communist times, when, as one of the first western organisations operating in Poland, it was seen as a 'window on the world'.

The BBC Polish service also benefits from a reputation established under the Communists, when it was one of only three non-state broadcasters in Poland. The BBC's perceived editorial independence was valued highly, even over the other international broadcasting networks available at the time: Voice of America and Radio Free Europe. The BBC continues to enjoy this high reputation, where the quality of its analysis is often rated more highly than the local Polish media. These days BBC Polish service current affairs programmes are broadcast on regional public radio, including a flagship 45-minute current affairs programme which reaches some 600,000 people, mostly in the BBC's 'cosmopolitans' target group. In addition, the BBC provides 5-minute hourly news bulletins on national and international news which are used by a number of commercial radio stations across the country. The result of all this exposure is that opinion surveys estimate that there are around 2.6 million 'conscious listeners' to the BBC.

This successful media footprint is one of the strongest aspects of the UK's relations with Poland, but two factors should be kept in consideration with regards to it. In the first place, the impact of the television station BBC World should not be overlooked, and as Poland's economy develops it is likely that it will become an even more influential, opinion-forming source of impression about the UK. Amongst the young professionals interviewed in 'Through Other Eyes', 29 per cent cited BBC World as their most important source for forming an opinion on the UK – ahead of BBC Polish Service radio (despite being broadcast in English), and second only to visiting the UK in person. In the important 'successor generation' group which that survey targeted, over 90 per cent of whom already speak English, BBC World's competition with CNN is an increasingly important area for attention. The second factor that should be considered in connection with the BBC's excellent profile in Poland is that there could be a danger of down-grading the importance of the service when Poland eventually does accede to the EU, taking the service down to the level of the BBC's involvement in Germany or in France. This would be to abandon all the advantages which had been gained in the first place.

Thus, British public diplomacy in Poland is very good, and covers particularly the long-term aspects of this important relationship well. However, there are some areas that would benefit from more attention. One of the most important constituencies which British public diplomacy in Poland must address, Polish farmers, is perhaps not being well covered by current efforts. This is because it can be hard to have an impact outside of metropolitan areas. It is vital for the UK to have some persuasive leverage with this group if it is to gain benefit from an alliance with Poland within the politics of the EU, and if Poland is to integrate efficiently into the structure of the new enlarged EU. British public diplomacy should be concerned with convincing the Polish that the CAP will be inflationary for food prices. It should also be concerned with convincing the Polish agricultural sector that a reformed CAP will benefit them by, for instance, providing funding for them to meet EU hygiene levels.

A second area where UK public diplomacy needs to be concentrating in the near future is in co-operation between political parties in the UK and Poland. The activities of the Westminster foundation, fostering parliamentary democracy and effective political parties in transition countries, mean that paradoxically we have better links with Polish political parties than with parties in most other EU countries. But as Poland rapidly approaches accession, we should begin to look at policy exchange and co-operation rather than the democratic capacity building with which the Westminster Foundation concerns itself. There is some work in this area. The British Council runs seminars which provide a forum for Polish policy-makers to discuss broad policy issues with UK counterparts and politicians from the Commission and other European countries. Recent seminars have covered themes like modernising government in Europe, EU enlargement and European integration. But a concerted bilateral programme of relationship-building would pay much greater dividends for the UK. This is an area where the Germans have been very active, and where their politically-oriented foundations, like the Konrad Adenhauer Stiftung and the Freidrich Ebert Stiftung, have been very effective at forging links with Poland's political class. Britain cannot afford to overlook this potentially very fruitful area.

Lastly, there is an important task for multilateral, EU level, public diplomacy to perform in Poland. It is by no means a certainty that the Polish referendum on accession will be won by the pro-Europeans. Given that enlargement has been decisively deemed to be in the interests of the current EU countries, it is also in their interests that the Polish referendum, and the other referenda, result in an enlargement, and consequently in their interests to combine their efforts to persuade the Poles to vote 'yes' to EU accession. The EU needs to act together to sell itself to the populations of the potential accession countries, just as the Irish government has to sell the benefits of enlargement and the Nice treaty to its own population, or the British government will have to sell benefits of joining the Euro to its sceptical population.

India

The India-UK relationship: strengths

Democratic system of government

Historic ties with Britain

Highly educated cosmopolitan urban minority

Internet use is increasing rapidly
- Internet users are currently estimated at 7 million

Economic ties are growing
- Trade of £5 billion per annum
- UK is the biggest investor in India
- 200 companies in sectors including biotechnology and IT
- 250 Indian firms have invested in the UK

Large Indian diaspora in the UK
- 1.3 million people of Indian descent in the UK
- Extensive family ties

Cricket is hugely popular

Large numbers of Indians visit the UK
- 200,000 visa applications each year

Burgeoning IT industry

Many UK NGOs active in India

The India-UK relationship: weaknesses

Only 3-4 per cent of the population knows English

Historic links with Britain are weakening
- The current political leadership is the last generation who experienced the British period

Nationalist political leadership with a dislike of foreign involvement in local and regional issues such as Kashmir

Suspicion of the strengthening of Pakistan's ties with the west

The Indian media is quick to criticise the UK

Negative reaction to the UK's support of the US after September 11th

UK public diplomacy in India

Strengths

Physical presence in the 4 major cities, and network of British libraries supported by the British Council in a further 7 cities

British Council is one of most modern and effective offices with pioneering Knowledge and Learning Centre

BBC World Service Hindi service is very popular in rural areas and has a good reputation

BBC World television is popular in urban areas among the growing number of people with satellite or cable television

Sponsored visits programme: 30 visits to the UK per year, including journalists, politicians and business people

Indian media are receptive to articles placed by the Embassy

High Commissioner's media appearances are well reported.

Weaknesses

predicted 25 million in 2005

No BBC World Service presence on FM due to high costs of FM frequencies

BBC Online in French is targeted not at France but at Francophone Africa

Foreign Office publications in English are of limited use in France

Journalists' visits not targeted at those already in the UK

Opportunities

Highly educated cosmopolitan urban minority

Burgeoning IT industry

Large NGO sector and high level of public awareness of social issues

Regionally influential

Huge population of over 1 billion people

Rapidly growing number of internet users: 5.5 million at the beginning of 2001, and a

Threats

Large rural population with low levels of literacy, particularly among women

Large number of languages spoken, with no one *lingua franca*

Large numbers of people have no access to media

Number of listeners to BBC World Service is falling

The UK's colonial links with India mean that it traditionally has a major institutional presence, and a considerable commitment of resources. The UK has a diplomatic presence in four major cities, and a British Council presence in a further seven. It undoubtedly spends more than any competitor country. But given the vast importance of India, and the scale of the public diplomacy challenge in communicating with it, those resources are meagre. India is the largest democracy in the world, with over 1 billion people. It has 28 states, 15 official languages, 24 languages spoken by a million people or more and up to 700 mutually unintelligible dialects. It has a GDP of $2.2 trillion, and a GDP growth rate of 6 per cent per annum in real terms. This amounts to a massively lucrative market, if it is ever fully opened up to international trade. In addition, it is a nodal player in WTO negotiation as a leader of the non-aligned movement, and as one of the world's most important transitional economies. It is a nuclear power, and is of pivotal regional and geopolitical importance. Along with Pakistan, it is the most likely candidate for first state to become involved in a nuclear war. It is one of China's chief regional rivals. Furthermore, its importance is bound to grow as it becomes more assertive internationally and more prosperous internally. It is, in short, one of the most important, and the most difficult, audiences for public diplomacy in the modern world.

The UK has a great variety of close links with India as a result of its colonial past. An estimated 4 per cent of the population speak English, and it is virtually a first language for many educated Indians. This small section of the population is in charge of many key sectors of society – economic, political and bureaucratic. There is a great deal of familiarity on both sides, stemming from the education of many of the Indian elite in the UK, and from the large Indian diaspora in Britain. However, that close relationship is under threat. A new generation of Indian leaders is emerging who have had no direct relations with the UK, and no experience of colonial rule. As India becomes richer, a growing entrepreneurial middle class is pushing out the old administrative elite. An increasing number of Indian MPs no longer speak English. In the British Council's *Through Other Eyes* survey of 'successor generation' young professional Indians, the UK lagged behind the US in both familiarity ratings and favourability ratings. This demonstrates that the UK faces a demographic threat to its public diplomacy position in India.

On top of this, India has a vast and sophisticated media market. It has more quality English-language national broadsheets then the UK does, and this despite the noted fact that the overwhelming proportion of the population cannot read English. It is estimated to have over 300 English language dailies, and over 2000 dailies in Hindi. Estimates of the total number of publications, including weeklies, monthlies, quarterlies and other journals in all languages in India place the figure at almost 40,000. Covering this vast media market is something of a tall order for the approximately 20 staff engaged in Press and Public Affairs work in the British diplomatic representations around India. These figures are an indication that public diplomacy in India could undoubtedly use more resources.

The UK is generally clear about the messages it wants to convey in India. It seeks to emphasise its commitment to India, its own status as an innovative and modern multicultural country, and as a major player in world affairs (a member of the UN Security Council, the EU and NATO etcetera). There is a mixed record on the effective transmission of these messages. One particular area that has not come across effectively is the presentation of the UK as a tolerant and multicultural society. There has been a positive reaction to British Council initiatives like the visit of Benjamin

Zephaniah to talk about the Stephen Lawrence case, and so demonstrate an openness in Britain about its race problems, but in the *Through Other Eyes* survey quoted above, racism and racial discrimination was the second most commonly listed weakness of the UK, behind an over-reliance on the United States.

But there are some key messages that the UK does not seek to put across with its public diplomacy in India which ought to be important aspects of that strategy. The promotion of regional security is a vital part of the UK's (and the world's) interest in South Asia. Public diplomacy can play an important part in this by, for instance, presenting the arguments for multilateralising the Kashmir conflict, and seeking to ease tensions between Muslims and Hindus in the region. More broadly, it is important to communicate to the Indian population the existence of an alternative route to international influence. At the moment, the message which the world sends to India by its actions and by its responses to Indian actions suggests that the only way to achieve recognition of India's strength – symbolised by a permanent seat on the UN Security Council, a luxury that China enjoys but which India is denied – is through the flexing of nuclear and other military muscles. There is a job for public diplomacy to do, which it does not currently take on either multilaterally or on a bilateral UK-Indian basis, in communicating that an alternative route via international co-operation, trade and engagement exists.

The second large area where public diplomacy ought to be contributing in India, but is not doing enough, is on the issue of globalisation and liberalisation of trade. The UK, along with the WTO countries as a whole, makes little effort to sell the advantages of free trade, and the Doha agreement, to the broader Indian population. Given that the enormous potential of the Indian market can only be tapped if its trade regulations are relaxed, and that this will only happen if a broad enough coalition of support can be built up within India's enormous demos, then strategic communication on the benefits of trade already being realised (including the powerful Indian IT industry) and on the potential gains from globalisation in the future, would be of great advantage to the UK. Although there is much work done with businessmen, promoting the UK as a trade partner and gateway to Europe, there are few attempts to engage the broader population in a consensus of support for trade liberalisation as a vision for India's future.

British public diplomacy in India covers the three dimensions of public diplomacy well, but there are important gaps and areas of under-resource that need to be highlighted.

In terms of short-term news management, the Embassy is faced with an enormous task with only a comparatively small staff, as noted above. Nevertheless, the coverage of the media is patchy and can be improved. The Embassy only really covers the English newspapers and the major publications in Hindi. Prior to September 11th, papers in Urdu were not even monitored, and even after their inclusion, there remain 13 official languages whose publications are not monitored. Because of the sensitivity of the Indian media to bad British news stories and government slip-ups – particularly events like the race riots in Bradford and Oldham in the summer of 2001 – swift reaction to news stories is especially important. Yet much of the public diplomacy output of the Embassy and consulates remains in English (in contrast to the US, which is able to do a lot of work in the various vernaculars), and the Embassy is concerned that more needs to be done by the government departments in Whitehall to instrumentalise the Indian press corps in London in rebutting negative impressions of the UK.

Another important consideration at the level of news management and news coverage is the position of the World Service in India, particularly with reference to the rising class of young entrepreneurial Indians which must be the chief target group of British public diplomacy strategy. The World Service's editorial independence enjoys a good reputation, as does its recognised expertise in the region in comparison with the American outlets. It also received a big boost in audience and prestige in the aftermath of September 11th when it was considered to be informative, unbiased and objective. But outside of this unfortunate and exceptional situation, most of the time the younger generation prefer to watch their news on television rather than listen to it on the radio. The BBC World Service did not come in the top ten of sources for impressions of Britain in the *Through Other Eyes* survey, whereas the television-based platform BBC World came in fifth. In fact, India is one country where BBC World is performing very well, and actually outperforms CNN by a factor of 3 to 1. Whilst it is clear that radio is the vital medium for communicating to India's rural poor, in terms of efficient return of influence on investment it must be recognised that India – a country with 70 million television sets – is increasingly a country where television is the vital medium for producing impact.

In the medium term, there are examples of inspired thinking on message delivery in Indian public diplomacy. When the England cricket team toured India under the captaincy of Nasser Hussain – an Englishman of Indian descent – the opportunity for a series of positive news stories on the inclusive multicultural nature of modern Britain was spotted and exploited. This was particularly influential given the enormously high profile of the sport of cricket in India, and indeed because of its pre-existing status as a highly politically charged game due to the frequently stormy and competitive India-Pakistan matches. In fact, a member of the Embassy's staff was assigned to the tour full time for the purposes of managing its public diplomacy potential.

Equally, the British Council and the Foreign Office have used the Indian diaspora in the UK well to put across the same strategic message. The Foreign Office's visits to the Punjabi community in Southall have strengthened links with that community and are to be publicised in India. There has also been attention paid to the nuanced issue of common perceptions of the British Indian diaspora as uneducated, unskilled and unambitious – a verdict often accompanied by unfavourable contrasts with the Silicon Valley millionaire stereotype of the Indian diaspora in the United States. British Indian dot.com millionaires are to figure heavily in future diplomatic visits.

Long-term relationship-building is also generally very good. The British Council manages to reach an audience of approximately 200,000 people a year, mostly through its network of information centres and libraries and its provision of English-language books and information. It hopes to increase that figure to 300,000 by concentrating on expanding internet-based but assisted distance learning. India is a priority country for the expansion of Chevening scholarships, and the target is to increase the number of Indians studying in the UK from 4,300 currently to around 10,000 in 2005. The Embassy's sponsored visits programme, which is followed up with interviews and often also results in positive news stories from media visitors, is another good model for developing the kind of links that can be very influential over the longer term. For instance, Prime Minister Vajpayee had been on a sponsored visit to the UK whilst in opposition. However, the scale of the programme – c.30 visitors in 2001 – is inadequate given the size of the population and of the governing class in India.

Co-ordination between the UK public diplomacy institutions in India works relatively well. The British Council and the Embassy have a good working relationship and complement one another's work well. But there are weaknesses of co-operation, particularly with the Department for International Development, in terms of co-ordination with the EU and other EU governments on messages of common interest.

The issue of using DFID work to public diplomacy advantage is a thorny one. Foreign Aid's chequered history of neo-colonial meddling and export promotion was the motivation behind DFID's avowed principle to concentrate exclusively on poverty reduction as its goal, and not to engage in any accompanying branding or public relations work whatsoever. Furthermore, given that some of the important development work that DFID engages in is not necessarily immediately popular (initiatives like putting in water meters, although highly beneficial in the long-term, can provoke powerful immediate negative reactions), there are occasions when public affairs work around such projects could actually be counter-productive, and could even work to undermine the legitimacy of the kind of reforming governments with whom DFID works. However, it is inescapable that the only UK government agency that has impact and reach outside of the metropolitan elite, and which does a great deal of very positive work, is DFID; and DFID acts entirely below the radar of public exposure. There must be a happy medium between a USAID model of brashly branding every cent and every brick of aid, and DFID's trappist silence. Perhaps by focusing on the positive outcomes of UK development work, a very important message could get across to a large number of Indians that the UK is engaged with and investing in the future of India, without compromising the work that DFID does.

The other main issue in public diplomacy co-operation in India is multilateral co-operation with the EU. India, as one of the nodal countries in trade negotiation, is one of those countries where the EU is very active diplomatically. There is good co-operation between the member states through the EU in areas like cultural presentation. But the wide interests of the European countries – in human rights, in good governance, and in forging consensus in favour of globalisation – are not areas where there has been a concerted attempt at combining mutually enforcing messages. EU public diplomacy should not just be limited to film festivals and cultural exchange, but should exploit a comparative multilateral advantage in dealing with hard political issues without the baggage that might go with such messages in a delicate post-colonial bilateral relationship like that of the UK and India.

Lastly, it is important to note the swiftly growing importance of the Internet as a platform for message delivery in India. India had 5.5 million internet users in 2001, and that figure is set to quintuple in 4 years to a predicted 25 million in 2005. This internet boom, linked to the strength of the Indian information technology sector as a whole, is concentrated around precisely the kind of successor generation Indians that UK public diplomacy seeks to target. The Embassy and the British Council have responded well to this changing situation. The Embassy's website, recently redesigned, attracts 1.8 million hits a month, and rising. This compares very well with, for instance, the Observer Online which is one of the UK's most frequently visited web pages at around 1 million a month. The Council has concentrated heavily on converting its English language teaching and information provision sources – the central relationship building tools – to a partially online basis, and aims to increase its reach by a half through this medium. The World Service has recently launched major multimedia websites in Hindi and Urdu, providing 24 hour news through text, graphics and streaming audio.

South Africa

The South Africa-UK relationship: strengths

South Africa is important to the UK for its strategic importance and influence in sub-Saharan Africa

The two countries have a longstanding relationship with many close personal contacts, including between the current South African political leadership and former anti-apartheid campaigners in the UK

Economically, the UK is by far the biggest investor in South Africa, and one of its most important trading partners

Opinions of the UK among young educated South Africans are generally favourable: in a survey conducted in 1999, the UK was rated highly for its economic stability, democracy, legal system, multicultural society, and for the quality of its higher education

Approximately two-fifths of educated young South Africans have visited the UK at least once

DFID and many UK NGOs are active in South Africa

The South Africa-UK relationship: weaknesses

The history of the UK's relations with South Africa, particularly the UK's ambivalent attitude to sanctions during the apartheid era, has left a feeling of mistrust among some

Differences between the two governments in their handling of the March 2002 Zimbabwe election also created wider public distrust

The major investment by the UK in South Africa is not widely recognised outside the business community, and companies which have been in South Africa for many years such as Shell and BP have come to be thought of as South African rather than British

In the 1999 survey quoted above, educated young South Africans thought of the UK as traditional, conservative and lacking in global perspective, and rated it significantly behind the US, Japan and Germany in terms of its scientific and technological innovation

Only 6 per cent of the black population attend university, and the majority of young South Africans have little contact with or understanding of the UK

UK public diplomacy in South Africa

Strengths	Weaknesses
Strengths Commitment to cooperative working among UK agencies, and joint mission statement Strengthening and refocusing of British Council and High Commission public diplomacy activity BBC World popular on satellite TV, and BBC news bulletins and foreign correspondents' reports used on public and commercial radio Market research and evaluation data collected by British Council	increased demand for education and training opportunities, international networking and information **Weaknesses** DFID does not have a public communications strategy for its work, and is not widely recognised outside its immediate circle of contacts
Opportunities Interest in British culture and sport, particularly among the young. Skills shortages and the need for capacity building create a demand for international expertise NEPAD provides an agreed framework for capacity building and development activity Emergence of a growing black professional class creates	**Threats** Reduction in British Council funding Barriers to development including the HIV/Aids crisis threaten South Africa's future development Instability and economic crisis in Zimbabwe could threaten South Africa's economic success

South Africa is a pivotally important country on the African continent – a growing economy and undoubtedly the pre-eminent regional power. Partly as a result of this importance, and partly as an accident of former colonial ties, South Africa enjoys a sizeable British presence: a large number of consulates for the High Commission, a large British Council effort, a lot of DFID development projects across the country and a significant number of British companies investing in it. It consequently has a greater concentration of British public diplomacy actors than those of many other countries and a correspondingly large commitment of resources that balances well with the importance of South Africa to the UK.

The UK has three main messages in South Africa. Firstly it seeks to put across an economic message, that the UK is the natural business partner and ally for South Africa. Second, it has an important message seeking to promote democracy and regional stability in Southern Africa – a message complicated by events in Zimbabwe surrounding Robert Mugabe's re-election. The British High Commission Mission Statement in South Africa states that, "We believe that Britain's single biggest interest in South Africa and the region is that the country should be successful, stable, prosperous and a positive influence." This leads on to the UK's final message which is that the UK's contributions to Southern African politics, and its relationship with the country in general, is unselfish – post-colonial not neo-colonial.

The UK's economic message seems to have got across to South Africans well. The UK is by far the largest investor in South Africa, and one of its most important trading partners, and this makes an effective base for a narrative that has the UK in the role of South Africa's chief economic ally. UK investment in South Africa was valued at £6.5 billion at the end of 1999, and the UK is South Africa's second largest export market and third largest source of imports. The extent of this economic partnership is recognised to an extent by the young urban South Africans interviewed by the British Council. They were among the most inclined to see the UK both as a key financial centre, and as the home of 'world-beating companies' – a sign that the UK's economic public diplomacy is on firm ground in South Africa. The other messages – the UK's unselfish interests, particularly in promoting regional stability – have perhaps been less successful. One test of the success of this kind of public diplomacy is the extent to which it can soften reactions to British statements that touch on the sensitivities these strategic messages are designed to address. South Africa's frosty response to British condemnation of the 'election' in Zimbabwe demonstrated that an inclination to see the British as 'meddling' had not been overcome.

Lying behind these challenges to British public diplomacy impact is a growing demographic challenge to British relations with South Africa, similar in kind to the threat posed by the rising generation of middle class leaders in India. Warm opinions of the UK, and the positive reputation of the British Council in particular, are based in part on links built up during the years of apartheid. The British Council made a considerable reputation for itself during the apartheid years, partly through its work in bringing disadvantaged black South Africans to the UK for higher education, and partly through its close relations with anti-apartheid campaigners – symbolised by its move from Pretoria, then a bastion of apartheid, to Johannesburg in 1987. The UK was a common place of refuge for Black leaders at that time and several ANC safe houses were maintained in London. This positive image was reinforced further when the Labour government came to power in 1997, and former anti-apartheid campaigners from Britain and also from South Africa now had seats on the UK government front bench.

But the generation that had direct experience of beneficial links with the UK are increasingly giving way to one that has no memory of such ties. One estimate puts 43 per cent of the South African population under the age of 19. The vast majority of this younger generation have had little or no experience of the UK, and display decreased interest in it as a result. UK public diplomacy institutions in South Africa, particularly the British Council, are well aware of the threat this generational change poses to UK-South African relations. The British Council's strategy in South Africa concentrates on engaging the successor generation in its activities, and particularly to impress upon them that the UK is a diverse and innovative country that is a source of opportunities for them.

The British public diplomacy institutions in South Africa in general work together well. This is at least in part a result of the High Commissioner's personal emphasis on the importance of public diplomacy, which she has been keen to place at the top of the agenda. In order to co-ordinate the work of the organisations and avoid duplication, 'task forces' of High Commission, DFID and British Council staff have been set up for a number of sectors in which the three institutions are involved such as HIV/Aids, conflict prevention and governance. These issue-led organisational units also act as channels of information and communication, and represent a good model for public diplomacy co-operation.

DFID are, however, unwilling to engage in broad public communications work as it is not considered to be part of their remit. This means that much of the UK's contribution to South Africa – some £30 million a year – comes to the attention primarily of a small number of stake-holders in government and NGOs who are directly involved with DFID work. This means that some opportunities for excellent public diplomacy work go begging, particularly as the message which such development work sends is a very positive one of the UK's engagement with South Africa's needs, and its difficult transformation programme. Where DFID projects do get wider publicity, this is generally either due to a high-profile visit by a UK visitor or the High Commissioner, which is publicised by the High Commission's own Press and Public Affairs Section, or because it is publicised by the project management agency itself, which may not necessarily even be British.

The final aspect worth highlighting in regard to UK public diplomacy in South Africa is the advantages that have accrued from a policy of hiring local, professional staff in communications roles. Both the High Commission and the British Council have put significant management changes in place over the last year, which build up their public relations and communications resources. On the British Council's part, this was partly in response to a cut in its core grant and partly to redirect resources into programmes, but also to free up resources to put in place an upgraded communications strategy. The changes have included: a move to new, smaller premises, with enquiries, information services and teaching all handled either electronically or off-site; a reduction in the number of UK expatriate staff by over half, replacing them with senior South African staff with professional experience and good networks of contacts, including a dedicated communications manager; and an improved website with far more information available on-line. The High Commission has also upgraded its staffing, upgrading the head of section and recruiting several new local staff with experience in the South African media. It has opened a new wing in the High Commission dedicated to press and public affairs work. This coincided with the relocation of the section from Cape Town to Pretoria, where it is close to the government and to Johannesburg where most media organisations are based.

This institutional change has resulted, for the Council at least, in improved communications networks and an excellent media strategy. The Council's employment of a communications professional who had previously worked in the President's Office and on the South African Olympic bid has produced an exemplary media strategy, aimed primarily at multiplication of impact, where even seminars aimed at elite participants are designed around hooks to secure media coverage and hence raise awareness of the UK in the broader successor generation audience as well as impacting on the small membership of the 'authority generation'. In terms of networking, the Council's links with black leaders, maintained through the Thatcher era, are now paying dividends. A situation where former ANC people are now employed by the British Council cannot but help in the creation of influential networks through which UK public diplomacy can work.

United Arab Emirates (UAE)

The United Arab Emirates - UK relationship: Strengths

The UK has strong historical links with the United Arab Emirates

Many Emiratis have personal experience of studying, living or visiting the UK

English is foreign language of choice for Emiratis

UK higher education is rated highly for its quality

The UAE is the UK's largest trading partner in the Gulf

A large number of British companies are based in the UAE, providing oil-related and other services

The British are the largest Western expatriate community in the UAE

British companies have a reputation for trustworthiness and high quality

The British Business Group, which has branches in Abu Dhabi and Dubai, is the largest national business group within the UAE

The decision of UK companies to keep their expatriate employees in the country after September 11th, in contrast to many US companies, was taken as a sign of the UK's continued trust and engagement with the UAE

The UK receives a lot of coverage in the Emirati press, most of it positive

The United Arab Emirates - UK relationship: weaknesses

The UK is considered not to be doing enough to resolve the Israel-Palestine situation

Many Emiratis feel the BBC is biased in favour of Israel in its reporting of the Israel-Palestine situation

Due to fears of racial attack in the UK, there has been a drop in numbers of Emiratis travelling there since September 11th

The US is more attractive than the UK to many young Emiratis because of its modern, state-of-the-art image and familiarity from US television programmes, and it is seen as the country of choice for work opportunities in sectors such as IT

UK public diplomacy in the United Arab Emirates

Strengths	**Weaknesses**
Good market research by the British Council	Lack of sufficient Arabic language skills among expatriate staff
Co-location of the BTA within the British Council in Dubai	No UK alumni association
British Business Groups in both Dubai and Abu Dhabi	No arts or cultural programme
British Tourist Authority college projects	
Regular trade missions	
English language teaching	
Information on study in the UK	
Arabic and English language BBC services	
Prince of Wales Business Initiative Forum Lectures	
Opportunities	*Threats*
Creation of 'Media City' in Dubai with regional influence	Young Emiratis tend to look to the US not the UK as the preferred country to visit or live in
Satellite dishes, owned in 67 per cent of households in 1997, are unrestricted by government	Low rating of UK academic qualifications in BTA tourism project survey
Large and increasing number of internet subscribers	Increasing competition for education provision in UAE, particularly for women
Creation of Dubai International Financial Centre	
'Emiratisation' policy leads to increased need for skills training of Emiratisprofessional class creates increased demand for education and training opportunities, international networking and information	

UK public diplomacy in the United Arab Emirates (UAE) is concentrated on securing advantage to what are considered the UK's overall interests in the UAE: firstly, to have a good friend to the UK in the Arab league, and secondly to maintain and strengthen the considerable commercial links between the two countries (the UAE is the UK's largest trading partner in the Gulf, and British business has a high-profile presence in the UAE, particularly in the oil industry). In order to further these interests, UK public diplomacy concentrates on the comparatively small Emirati population in the UAE. Although the Emirati minority makes up only 10-20 per cent of the population, it makes up a very large proportion of the 20 per cent who are citizens, and is by far the wealthiest section. However, while the Embassies aim to maintain good relationships with the UAE's political and business leaders, this group is restricted to a small number of powerful families, limiting the amount of influence that public diplomacy has on this group. As a result, the main public diplomacy focus of all the organisations is the younger generation of Emiratis.

This focus means that the British Council's education services are one of the key tools of public diplomacy in the UAE. There is a big demand for education services for the young generation of Emiratis. This is partly because wealthy Emirati parents are keen for their children to know English and to study abroad, partly as a consequence of a policy of 'Emiratisation' in local businesses, which is increasing the need for skills training for young Emiratis. In addition, there is increasing demand for better higher education opportunities in the UAE, for those who do not wish to travel abroad or whose parents do not wish them to – particularly women. The large size of many Emirati families – making overseas education an expensive option – and security fears following September 11th reinforce this tendency.

On the whole, British education is in high demand, but a recent BTA survey suggested that British academic qualifications may no longer be valued as highly as in the past, making the work of promoting UK universities and educational products all the more important.

The British Council provide English language teaching and other professional courses in its four teaching centres in Abu Dhabi, Dubai, Sharjah and Ras Al Khaimah.

Information and advice on opportunities for study in the UK is provided in British Council information centres in Dubai and Abu Dhabi, on the British Council website, and through travelling exhibitions to higher educational colleges, and the period 1998 to 2002 saw a considerable increase in student numbers.

The British Council is responding to the demand for improved educational opportunities in the UAE through offering assisted distance learning courses from UK universities: Strathclyde University's MBA and Newcastle University's MEd in TESOL are both available at the Dubai British Council, and the MEd will be available in Abu Dhabi in the future. New Distance learning courses are also being developed on-line. A new initiative is the opening the new Dubai British University offering full-time British higher education for those who do not wish to go overseas.

There is considerable scope and demand for training among Emirati professionals. The British Council runs English language and professional development training contracts for a range of private and public sector organisations, including the Abu Dhabi National Oil Company (ADNOC), hotels, police, armed forces, and local government. It also offers general and business English courses at its teaching centres

The creation of the Dubai International Financial Centre in February 2002 creates interesting new opportunities for engagement by the UK, for example through skills development and work exchanges to the UK.

A joint initiative of the Prince of Wales Business Initiative Forum (POWBIF) and the British Business Group is a series of lectures to higher education colleges on corporate social responsibility, given by British companies such as BP. These created a lot of enthusiasm both for British corporate practice, and for the companies themselves.

The second key tool of British public diplomacy in the UAE is the media. The BBC World Service has recently boosted its Arabic output to a 24-hour stream for the region. Also, the BBC Arabic website is a market leader in the region, currently registering some 8 million page impressions per month, a significant proportion of which originate in UAE. Although the Emirati media are highly controlled, they are nonetheless influential as a source of information on the UK. Most print media are based in Dubai. Television is also very influential as a source of news and information, with major television stations based in Dubai, Abu Dhabi, and in other emirates of the UAE. Al-Jazeera, based in Qatar, is also much watched and highly influential in the UAE.

One feature of the very controlled local media is the importance it places on stories concerning its political leaders and members of its ruling families. This tends to multiply the positive or negative effects of state and VIP visits. This played negatively during President Sheikh Zayid's recent visit to the UK, when he failed to meet Tony Blair – and conversely, Tony Blair's visit to him in Geneva in late 2001 (after September 11th) was seen as a major signal of continued friendship between the two countries.

The Embassy Press and Public Affairs Sections are able to use this attention to VIPs to their advantage, by inviting leading Emiratis to important UK occasions, thus ensuring positive media coverage.

In terms of stories originating in London, such as key UK government speeches, it is unfortunately often difficult for these to be placed in the local media. This is due to delays in getting Arabic translations and by the difference in the UK and Arabic working weeks – the UAE working week runs from Saturday to Wednesday, so a story held over the UK weekend from Friday to be sent out on Monday arrives in the UAE several working days after the speech was made.

After September 11th the Embassy Press and Public Affairs Section focused on the message that UK is multiracial and a friend of the Muslim world. A number of high-level visits in both directions shortly after the crisis were of major importance in reinforcing this message. In October, the Abu Dhabi National Oil Company (ADNOC) trade mission to the UK helped to persuade others that it was still safe to visit the UK. And in November, trade missions from the UK to the UAE, including a visit by the Duke of York in his new role as foreign representative for trade and investment, and a display by the Red Arrows, were widely seen as a positive message about the UK's continued engagement in the Gulf and in the UAE.

However, the generally effective public diplomacy work of the UK institutions in the UAE does not, perhaps, hold in sufficiently clear view the fact that the UK's key relationship with the UAE is not just bilateral, aimed at gaining influence within the UAE and with its citizens, but is instead through the UAE's media outlets to the rest of the Arab World. The opening of Dubai's 'Media City' in February 2000 is a concrete demonstration that the UAE represents a nodal point of communication with a much broader Arab Muslim population that the West has a vital interest in influencing. A number of major media organisations – such as Reuters, Sony, Zen TV, Middle East Business News and other major broadcasters have opened offices in Dubai, and the largest Middle East pan-Arab broadcaster, MBC, has decided to relocate there from London. Given the importance of broadcast TV, particularly pan-Arab satellite broadcasting like MBC, in forming Arab opinions about foreign policy in general and relations with the West in particular, this grouping of media organisations represents a clear opportunity for reaching a very broad and very important audience.

Some work has been done in this regard. The Head of the Islamic Media Centre in London visited Abu Dhabi and was interviewed by Abu Dhabi TV. Unfortunately, few British appear on Al-Jazeera due to a lack of those with sufficient Arabic language skills, although it has been a central target of much of the Coalition's ad hoc public diplomacy effort after September 11th. But attempts to put across the Western point of view to Arab populations via Dubai's media organisations ought to be a co-operative Western effort backed by the institutions and resources necessary to operate a permanent presence on those media. This opportunity for influencing the pan-Arab television news agenda would be an excellent starting point for international co-operation on public diplomacy (see Chapter 4 of this report). At the least there should be an EU public diplomacy unit seeking to place qualified interviewees on the Arab television stations, backed by EU money, and putting across from a broad Western standpoint the kinds of messages – of diversity and religious tolerance, that fighting terrorism is not the same as making war on Islam and is in the interests of Arab as well as Western nations – that are currently seen to be of such import to communicate to the Arab World.

Appendix II: Niche Diplomacy
How Norway uses scarce resources to punch above its weight

1. Overview

Norway's international footprint is relatively small. It is a small country of under 5 million people. Although a member of NATO, it is not a member of the EU. This leaves it on the fringe of European decision-making on many issues which have a direct effect upon it. In addition to this initial unpromising position, it lacks many of the features that have helped other small countries have an impact on the world stage. Norwegian is not an international language, and is spoken by large populations nowhere outside Norway. Geographically, Norway is not a 'hub' country like Belgium or the Netherlands, and does not have much opportunity to build up familiarity through travel and tourism. It lacks any strong brands or international companies to raise awareness of Norwegian business. It does not have a strong popular culture that exports well. Prima facie, therefore, Norway should have difficulty gaining an international profile.

Yet, Norway has a voice and presence on the international stage out of proportion to its modest position and unpromising assets. It has achieved this presence through aggressive pursuit of niche public diplomacy, and a ruthless prioritisation of its target audiences. Norway's concentration on a single message – Norway as a force for peace in the world – and on ameliorating the effect of two negative images – lack of influence in Europe through non-EU status and attachment to whaling – has allowed it to communicate much more effectively than countries like the

UK, which can have a confusing maelstrom of perhaps conflicting messages. Equally, its geographical concentration of the vast majority of its public diplomacy activity on just 6 key relationships – the USA, Russia, France, Germany, the UK and Japan – has allowed it to produce the international impact it has on a small budget of just under £5 million.

Norway's prime goal in securing this international visibility around the issue of peace and conflict prevention is twofold. Firstly, it does allow Norway to gain a general profile it might not already have which is beneficial to the country in broad terms. More specifically though, Norway's reputation in conflict resolution ensures that it is regarded as relevant in multilateral forums, and by other important international players, and this affords it influence on this issue.

2. Strategy

Main features:

a. Concentration of public diplomacy resources *vis a vis* six countries with great bilateral importance to Norway, i.e. the US, UK, France, Germany, Japan and Russia (where Russia and the US relationships are crucial security ones; the UK, Germany & France are the 3 most powerful EU states; all bar Russia are key economic interests; and Russia affects Norway's border region). Washington, London, Berlin, and Paris all have expatriate staff heading up a public affairs unit. There are also dedicated staff in Copenhagen, Stockholm and Helsinki, but with much smaller budgets as these are not priority countries, and in a sense can be regarded as part of the 'home market' (most projects and exchange are based on individual and institution contacts). In other Embassies, information and cultural work is handled by local staff or diplomats who also have other responsibilities.

b. Positioning as a contributor to world peace enables Norway to achieve greater visibility than its size would otherwise warrant and rebuts accusations of isolationism. Main activities in this field are conflict resolution activity in the Middle East (the Oslo Accord, etc.) Sri Lanka and elsewhere, and Norway's large aid budget. Norway also operates a 'rapid-reaction force' to assist in election monitoring and conflict prevention – The Norwegian Resource Bank for Democracy and Human Rights (NORDEM) – that manages to operate in around 20 countries annually. The closeness of NORDEM's co-operation with OSCE further emphasises Norway's contribution to peace with key allies. Norway also try to play a role on a regional basis, i.e. in the Barents region, in fostering economic and social development and environmental cooperation in North West Russia. The Nobel Peace Prize originating in Oslo is a happy historical fact which gives Norway a widely recognised peg to hang this side of its story on. Future plans include setting up a Peace Institute in Norway.

c. Norway seeks to rebut and/or avoid negative publicity on whaling and on Norway's perceived isolationist stance (a perception coming out of its non-membership of the EU). It employs both proactive (news management, visits) and 'avoidance' (NOT mentioning whaling in the US) tactics.

3. Coordination overseas
Norwegian public diplomacy overseas is undertaken under a single banner, 'Team Norway,' which was adopted in the mid-90s to both encourage and describe the close cooperation overseas between Embassies, the Norwegian Tourist Board, the Norwegian Export Council, the Norwegian Seafood Export Council, Chambers of Commerce and, in the US, the Norwegian Information Service. Originally a closely-integrated strategic

approach, it now describes a looser cooperation and sharing of information, with each organisation working to its own targets but linking with the other organisations' activity where appropriate. In the US, Team Norway organisations on the East Coast meet every 7-8 weeks, with semi-annual meetings for Team Norway organisations in the whole country. The phrase 'Team Norway' remains as a powerful slogan for member organisations.

4. Institutional Coordination in Norway

Up until a year ago, the promotion of Norwegian culture overseas was split between 3 ministries: the Ministry of Culture dealt with other Scandinavian countries; the Norwegian Agency for International Development Co-operation (NORAD) with developing countries and the Ministry of Foreign Affairs (MFA) with the remainder. Short term cultural exchange projects have now been moved to the MFA, but there is still a 2-way split between the MFA and the Ministry of Culture. The Ministry of Culture seems prepared to hand over responsibility for cultural promotion work in Scandinavian countries to the MFA, but the organisational change yet to be made. The Ministry of Culture also has an agency, Norsk Kulturrad (Norwegian Arts Council) which funds arts events , nationally, and which more and more finds itself involved in international projects. The Ministry of Culture has responsibility for funding the "import" side of international cultural projects, but has very little money allocated for this purpose, and mainly regard this as a task for the larger cultural institutions.

Within the MFA, there is a split between media-relations staff for the Ministers/State Secretaries who do day-to-day news management, and the Press & Cultural Affairs section who produce longer term information material, co-ordinate inward visits by journalists, etc.

Other organisations with an overseas remit or interest include the Ministry of Education & Research (for universities projects) and local government (some of which are very active in international exchanges).

There have been two proposals put on the table in recent years for improving the co-ordination between the different organisations. One was for the establishment of a 'Norwegian Council' along the lines of the Swedish or British Council. This has been turned down as too expensive (although the Swedish Council model is considerably cheaper than the British because it doesn't include overseas offices). The second (suggested in the Rudeng report) is for a co-ordinating body to be set up within the MFA responsible for press and cultural affairs. This has been agreed in principle, but has received no extra money, and therefore hasn't yet gone ahead. It is doubtful as to whether it will be effective as the Ministry of Culture is unwilling to be 'co-ordinated' by the MFA.

Cultural exchange activity is planned by sectoral committees of members of the arts community, co-ordinated by the MFA. Embassies can take initiatives, make recommendations or comment on plans, but are not the final decision-makers on which cultural performances or activities take place where. Some Embassies have a separate budget for public diplomacy purposes.

5. Activities

a. Idea of increased use of international networking, especially among the young (rather than the 'seminar-tired' older people already in influential positions.)

b. Visits by member of the Norwegian royal family often used for public diplomacy purposes.

c. Famous names as 'door openers' – i.e. Ibsen, Munch, Grieg used as pegs for introducing more contemporary artists. Also potential for using Nobel in peace/human rights fields.

d. Information campaign on informing young Norwegians about globalisation issues. (Information to Norwegians about foreign policy is part of MFA's role).

6. Major events

a. Norway 2005. 2005 will be the 100th anniversary of Norway's independence from Sweden, and a big domestic festival is being planned, which will also be reflected in activities overseas. Sweden's sensitivities will need careful handling. Message domestically will be internationalist and message internationally will be pro-peace.

7. Budget

Expenditure on Press, Culture & Information work:

2000 = NOK52.2m (c £4.3 m)

2001 = NOK57.2m (c £4.7 m)

(No increase in 2002)

Breakdown of 2000 expenditure (NOK):

Cultural activities	17 m
Info/PR activities abroad	17 m
Press activities	10 m
Teaching Norwegian abroad	6 m
Info to the Norwegian public	2.2 m (= 4.2 per cent, c £180k)
Total	**52.2m**

Appendix III: Global Brands

Brand	2001 Brand Value ($MM)	Country of origin
Bacardi	3,204	Bermuda
Bermuda total	3,204	
Carlsberg	1,075	Denmark
Denmark total	1,075	
Nokia	35,035	Finland
Finland Total	35,035	
L'Oreal	17,798	France
Danone	13,583	France
Louis Vuitton	7,053	France
Chanel	4,265	France
Moet & Chandon	2,470	France
France total	45,169	
Mercedes	21,728	Germany
BMW	13,858	Germany
Merck	9,672	Germany
Volkswagen	7,338	Germany
SAP	6,307	Germany
adidas	3,650	Germany
Nivea	1,782	Germany
Siemens	1,029	Germany
Germany total	65,363	
Guinness	1,357	Ireland
Ireland total	1,357	
Gucci	5,363	Italy
Armani	1,490	Italy
Benetton	1,002	Italy
Italy total	7,855	
Toyota	18,578	Japan
Sony	15,005	Japan
Honda	14,638	Japan
Nintendo	9,460	Japan
Canon	6,580	Japan
Panasonic	3,490	Japan
Japan total	67,752	
Samsung	6,374	Korea
Korea total	6,374	
Philips	4,900	Netherlands
Heineken	2,266	Netherlands
Netherlands total	7,166	
Ericsson	7,069	Sweden
IKEA	6,005	Sweden
Absolut	1,378	Sweden
Sweden total	14,452	
Nestle	41,688	Switzerland

Brand	2001 Brand Value ($MM)	Country of origin
Nescafe	13,250	Switzerland
Rolex	3,701	Switzerland
Swatch	1,004	Switzerland
Switzerland total	59,643	
Unilever	37,847	UK
Diageo	15,004	UK
Reuters	5,236	UK
BP	3,247	UK
Shell	2,844	UK
Smirnoff	2,594	UK
Johnnie Walker	1,649	UK
Financial Times	1,310	UK
UK Total	69,732	
Coca-Cola	68,945	US
Johnson & Johnson	68,208	US
Microsoft	65,068	US
IBM	52,752	US
P&G	45,435	US
Intel	34,665	US
Disney	32,591	US
Ford	30,092	US
McDonald's	25,289	US
AT&T	22,828	US
Marlboro	22,053	US
Citibank	19,005	US
Hewlett-Packard	17,983	US
Cisco Systems	17,209	US
American Express	16,919	US
Gillette	15,298	US
Merrill Lynch	15,015	US
Colgate-Palmolive	14,361	US
Compaq	12,354	US
Oracle	12,224	US
Budweiser	10,838	US
Kodak	10,801	US
Pfizer	8,951	US
Gap	8,746	US
Dell	8,269	US
Goldman Sachs	7,862	US
Nike	7,589	US
Heinz	7,062	US
Kellogg's	7,005	US
MTV	6,599	US
Pepsi	6,214	US
Xerox	6,019	US
Pizza Hut	5,978	US
Harley Davidson	5,532	US

Brand	2001 Brand Value ($MM)	Country of origin
Apple	5,464	US
KFC	5,261	US
Sun Microsystems	5,149	US
Kleenex	5,085	US
Colgate	4,572	US
Wrigley's	4,530	US
AOL	4,495	US
Yahoo!	4,378	US
Avon	4,369	US
Duracell	4,140	US
Boeing	4,060	US
Texas Instruments	4,041	US
Kraft	4,032	US
Motorola	3,761	US
Levi's	3,747	US
Time	3,724	US
Hertz	3,617	US
Tiffany & Co.	3,483	US
amazon.com	3,130	US
Burger King	2,416	US
Mobil	2,415	US
Wall St. Journal	2,184	US
Barbie	2,037	US
Polo Ralph Lauren	1,910	US
Fedex	1,885	US
Starbucks	1,757	US
Jack Daniels	1,583	US
Pampers	1,410	US
Hilton	1,235	US
GE	42,396	US
US total	858,024	

Appendix IV: the main interviewees for the project

In the UK:

Sir Michael Jay, Richard Stagg, John Buck, Carole Sweeney, Caroline Matthew, Tim Flear, Jane Clarke, Nicholas Armour, Patrick Holdich, Piers Cazalet, Bruce Bucknell, Philip Malone, Chris Henderson and colleagues at the FCO;

Baroness Helena Kennedy, David Green, Andrew Fotheringham, Patrick Spaven, and colleagues at the British Council.

Nigel Chapman, Fred Martenson, Barry Langridge, Jeff Hazell, Sam Miller, Sylvie Morot, Marek Cajzner, Grzegorz Paluch, and colleagues at the BBC Worldservie and BBC World.

H.E. Tarald Brautastet, Oyvind Stokke, and colleagues, Norwegian Embassy in London;

Ann Pearcey, Trade Partners UK and Steve Davies, Department of Trade and Industry

Tamsin Bailey, Design Council; Daniel Sreebny, US Embassy;

Alistair Campbell, 10 Downing Street;

Tucker Eskew, Co-alition Information Centre

In France:

Bruno Delaye, DGCID, Director General, Ministry of Foreign Affairs; Catherine Suard, Jean Garbe, Marie-Anna Lebovits, Patric, Donabedian, Ronald Goeldner, Olivier Richard, DGCID, Ministry of Foreign Affairs; John Tod, British Council France; Dany Cavelier and students at the Centre de formation des journalistes

Richard Lankford, US Embassy Press Office; Marit Hodanger, Norwegian Tourist Bureau; Dr Dieter Strauss, Director Goethe Institut; Richard Morgan, British Embassy; Ulrich Marthaler, Invest UK; John Gaudern, British Tourist Authority.

In India:

Edmund Marsden, Director British Council India and other British Council staff; James Callahan, Counsellor for Public Affairs, US Embassy; Yasuo Minemura, Counsellor for Information and Culture, Japanese Embassy; Thierry Audric, Counsellor for Cultural Affairs, French Embassy; Carles Lutyens, British Business Group; Tilmann Waldraff, Director Max Mueller Bhavan (Goethe Institute);

Heike Dettmann, Counsellor for Cultural Affairs, German Embassy; Christof Werr, Goethe Institut; Tom Macan, Deputy High Commissioner and staff at the British High Commission; Sukumar Muralidharan, Chief of Bureau, Frontline;

Chandralekha Roy, Editor, The Economic Times on Sunday; Robert Graham-Harrison, Director, and colleagues at DFID India; Francois Massoulie, First Secretary, European Commission; Arun Muttreja, Programme Director VSO India

Chevening programme alumni.

In Norway:

Eva Bugge, Rolf Willy Hansen, Arne Gjermundsen, Alf Modvar, Jan Gerhard Lassen, Johan Meyer, Espen Rikter Svendsen and colleagues at the Department for Press, Culture and Information, Ministry of Foreign Affairs; Jon Morland, Press Spokesman International Development, MFA; Iver Neumann, Department of European Policy Questions, MFA; Ole Jacob Bull, Jean Yves Gallardo and Christian Lund, Norwegian Cultural Council; Erik Rudeng and Mette Lending, authors of 'Change and Renewal' report; Janne Haaland Matlary, ARENA

Svein-Erik Ovesen, Norwegian Tourist Bureau; Bjorn Otto Sverdrup, Confederation of Norwegian Business and Industry; Kjetil Wiedswang, Dagens Naeringsliv; Jan Erik Raanes, Norge 2005; Nils Morten Udgaard, Aftenposten

Mr Alf Modvar and Ms. Margaretha Østern, Ministry of Culture; State Secretary Elspeth Tronstad, MFA

In Poland:

Tim Simmons, Counsellor and Deputy Head of Mission, British Embassy

Alicia Clyde, Press and Public Affairs Officer, British Embassy; Andrew C Koss, Counselor for Public Affairs, and Roy S Weatherston, US Embassy; Jerzy Roguski, Director American Information Resource Center; Oda von Breitenstein, Konrad Adenauer Stiftung; Ambassador Sten Lundbo, Norwegian Embassy; Michael Davenport, Trade Partners UK; Hanna Jezioranska, Delegation of the European Commission in Poland; Robert Kozak, BBC World Service; Jean-Yves Potel, French Embassy; Chevening programme alumni Agnieszka Ostrowska and Agnieszka Soltys;

In South Africa:

H.E. Ann Grant, British High Commission; Andy Sparkes, Nick Sheppard, Bob Thain, Randolph Jones, British High Commission; Judy Moon, US Embassy

Jim McAlpine and Hushe Mzenda, DFID Southern Africa; Judy Leon, Trade Partners UK; Philip Howell, Barclays Bank PLC; Roger Baxter, Chamber of Mines of South Africa; Ronnie Ntuli, Johannesburg Metropolitan Chamber of Commerce and Industry; Nick Ras and Gous Wilson, LawGibb Group

John Loos, ABSA; Clive Gobby, Director and Paul Johnson, Director Communications, British Council; Osamu Imai, Japanese Embassy

Charles Mabaso, Royal Netherlands Embassy; Johan Viljoen, French Embassy; ll Ishmael and Neil Carney, British Tourist Authority; Chevening programme alumni

In the United Arab Emirates:

(Abu Dhabi) Robert Sykes, Director British Council Gulf States; Robert Schwarz, British Business Group Abu Dhabi; Alistair McKenzie, John Gardner, Steve Davis and Jason Smith, British Embassy Abu Dhabi; (Dubai): Tim Gore, Director British Council Dubai; Jennifer Bibbings, British Business Group Dubai; Jonathan Walsh, Face to Face Public Relations; Simon Collis, Consul General, British Embassy Dubai; Mark Miller, British Tourist Authority; Dr Bassem Younes, University of Sharjah

Emirati students working at the British Council

In the US:

(in Washington DC); Sir Christopher Meyer, Ambassador;

Robert Peirce, British Embassy; Susan Stewart, First Secretary Scottish Affairs, British Embassy; Peter Smyth, Northern Ireland Bureau, British Embassy; Andy Mackay, Director British Council; Professor Barry Fulton, The George Washington University; Steven Livingston, The George Washington University; Mary Gawronski, Georgetown University; Anthony Quainton, National Policy Association; Ambassador Jurk Vollebek and Jon Age Oyslebo, Norwegian Embassy; Martin Turner, BBC Washington Bureau Chief; James Wilkinson, Coalition Information Centre, The White House; Ambassador Christopher Ross, State Department; Jefferson T Brown, David L Arnett, Joe B Johnson, Donna L Woolf of the State Department; Professor Joseph s. Nye, Dean Kennedy School of Government; Professor Benjamin Barber

(in Boston) Teresa Evans, British Consulate-General; Professor Alan Henrikson, Fletcher School of Law and Diplomacy, Tufts University; Professor Joseph Nye, Kennedy School of Government, Harvard University; Jane Christo and colleagues at WBUR-FM public radio; George Ferguson, HM Consul-General; Professor Peter Hall, Center for European Studies, Harvard University

(in New York)Sara Everett, British Information Services New York and colleagues; Sir Thomas Harris, HM Consul-General, New York; Robert Fletcher, M & C Saatchi; Paula Kerger and Beth Hope, Channel Thirteen/WNET; Ray Raymond, British Consulate-General; Atlantic and City Fellowship alumni

Colonel Jay Parker, West Point; David Tereschuk, consultant to the UN. Donn Rogosin and Kent H Steele, WLIW21 public television; Richard Fursland, British American Business Inc; Eva Vincent, Marianne Moe and Espen Gullikstad, Royal Norwegian Consulate General; Robert Titley, British Tourist Authority

FROM WAR TO WORK

Rowena Young

March 2002, £16.95, plus £1 p+p, ISBN 1 903558 07 7

Kindly supported by Globalegacy

'An insightful analysis that gets us beyond the anachronistic hard on/soft on drugs debate, and points up the key dilemmas facing governments in the search for an effective drug policy',

Mike Trace, National Treatment Agendy

THIRD GENERATION CORPORATE CITIZENSHIP

Simon Zadek

November 2001, £19.95, plus £1 p+p. ISBN 1-903558 08 5

Kindly supported by Diageo and Friends Ivory & Sime

'Zadek strikes at the heart of the debate.'

Craig Cohon, Global Legacy

The Pro-European Reader

Dick Leonard & Mark Leonard (editors) with essays by Winston Churchill, Jean Monnet, Roy Jenkins, Mikhail Gorbachev, Milan Kundera, David Puttnam and Tony Blair.

Published by Palgrave

November 2001, £16.99, ISBN 0 -333977211

'Here's a book full of cures for prejudice and phobia. Some of the antidotes are bold, some wry, some profound, some sharp – all short. The treatment is worth every Euro.'

Neil Kinnock

THE KIDNAPPING BUSINESS

Rachel Briggs
Kindly supported by Hiscox, Control Risks Group, ASM Ltd., Marsh Ltd. and SCR
March 2001, £14.95, plus £1 p+p

'A fascinating pamphlet', Simon Jenkins, The Times

THE FUTURE SHAPE OF EUROPE

Mark Leonard (editor)
Kindly supported by Adamson BSMG Worldwide
November 2000 £9.95; plus £1 p+p.

*'The Europe of Nice is a building site waiting for new
master builders. A booklet by The Foreign Policy Centre
makes the point more eloquently than any polemicist'*, Peter
Preston, The Guardian

NGO RIGHTS AND RESPONSIBILITIES:
A new deal for global governance

Michael Edwards, Director of Governance, Ford Foundation (writing personally)
In association with NCVO
July 2000 £9.95; plus £1 p+p. ISBN 0-9053558-00-X

'Compelling and succinct', Peter Hain, former Minister of State, FCO

GOING PUBLIC:
Diplomacy for the Information Society (interim report)

Mark Leonard and Vidhya Alakeson
May 16 2000 £9.95; plus £1 p+p. ISBN 0-9535598-7-4
The project is supported by the BBC World Service,
The British Council, and the Design Council.

'An important new pamphlet...argues that the old ideas of
British diplomacy must change profoundly',
Gavin Esler, The Scotsman

AFTER MULTICULTURALISM

Yasmin Alibhai-Brown, The Foreign Policy Centre
May 2000 £9.95; plus £1 p+p. ISBN 0-9535598-8-2

'Yasmin is brave, intelligent and always worth reading',
Diane Abbott, MP, New Statesman

RE-ENGAGING RUSSIA

John Lloyd, Journalist and Member of The Foreign Policy Centre's Advisory
Council
In association with BP Amoco
20th March 2000 £9.95; plus £1 p+p. ISBN 0-9535598-6-6

'Re-engaging Russia is excellent on where Russia's
relationships with the West went wrong...thought-
provoking, highly enjoyable, creative and timely',
Rt Hon Keith Vaz MP, Minister for Europe

REINVENTING THE COMMONWEALTH

Kate Ford and Sunder Katwala, The Foreign Policy Centre
In association with the Royal Commonwealth Society
November 1999 £9.95; plus £1 p+p. ISBN 0-9535598-4-5

'Intelligent and wide-reaching', **The Times**

'[The Centre's report has] very strong merits. Its proposals deserve honest enquiry', Business Day, South Africa 'My first thought was "Why has it taken 50 years to start this debate? Why aren't more developing countries leading it?"', **Sharon Chetty, The Sowetan**

TRADING IDENTITIES:
Why Countries and Companies Are Becoming More Alike

Wally Olins,
October 1999 £9.95; plus £1 p+p. ISBN 0-9535598-3-1

'A fascinating pamphlet', **Peter Preston, The Guardian**

GLOBALIZATION – KEY CONCEPTS

David Held & Anthony McGrew, David Goldblatt & Jonathan Perraton
April 12th 1999 £4.95, plus £1 p+p. ISBN 0-9535598-0-7

'An indispensable counterweight to optimists and pessimists alike', **Will Hutton**

'This is the agenda on which a new politics must be constructed and new alliances forged', **Clare Short, Secretary of State for International Development, New Statesman**

NETWORK EUROPE

Mark Leonard, The Foreign Policy Centre
In association with Clifford Chance
10th September 1999 £9.95; plus £1 p+p. ISBN 0-9535598-2-3

'A radical agenda for reform from the government's favourite foreign policy think-tank',
Stephen Castle, Independent on Sunday

'A welcome contribution to the important debate about Europe's future', **Rt Hon Tony Blair MP, Prime Minister**

THE POSTMODERN STATE AND THE NEW WORLD ORDER

Robert Cooper, Cabinet Office (writing in a personal capacity)

In association with Demos

2nd edition

What did 1989 really mean? Robert Cooper argues that the end of the Cold War also marked the end of the balance-of-power system in Europe. Yet today's open, multi-lateral postmodern states must deal with a complex world – where many states follow traditional realpolitik, while collapsed and failing states present the dangers of pre-modern chaos. The second edition of this groundbreaking pamphlet also addresses how the role of religion in international politics is very different today.

'Mr Cooper's pamphlet explains, lucidly and elegantly, how the emergence of what he calls the postmodern state has changed international relations', **New Statesman**

ALSO FORTHCOMING IN 2002

Mark Leonard and Catherine Stead on **Public Diplomacy: Comparative Experiences**

Mark Leonard, Sacha Chan Kam and Phoebe Griffith on **Immigration , Integration and Citizenship** (kindly supported by The Employability Forum)

Rachel Briggs on **Travel Advice**

Yasmin Alibhai-Brown, David Blunkett, Michael Wills, David Lammy, Philip Dodd Professor Francesca Klug and others on **Global Britons: Reflections on identity after Oldham, Bradford and September 11th**

Adrienne Katz on **Identity and Young People**

Francesca Klug on **Human Rights**

Need to Know, a novel by Narration

Christopher Haskins on **The Future of European Agriculture**

See www.fpc.org.uk for news and information.
Write to mail@fpc.org.uk to join our email list
For subscriptions and partnership scheme, see overleaf

Subscribe to The Foreign Policy Centre

The Foreign Policy Centre offers a number of ways for people to get involved. Our subscription scheme keeps you up-to-date with our work, with at least six free publications each year and our quarterly newsletter, Global Thinking. Subscribers also receive major discounts on events and further publications.

Type of Subscription	Price
☐ Individuals	£50
☐ Organisations	£150
☐ Corporate and Libraries (will receive ALL publications)	£200

Please make cheques payable to **The Foreign Policy Centre**, indicating clearly your postal and email address and the appropriate package, and send to Subscriptions, The Foreign Policy Centre, Mezzanine Floor, Elizabeth House, 39 York Road, London SE1 7NQ. For further details, contact Rachel Briggs: rachel@fpc.org.uk

The Foreign Policy Centre Diplomatic Forum

The Foreign Policy Centre Diplomatic Forum is aimed at the key embassy players. It is an ideal way for embassies to keep up-to-date with the work of The Foreign Policy Centre and will provide a useful environment for ideas sharing.

Members will receive the following benefits:

- Special invitations to attend The Foreign Policy Centre annual Diplomatic Forum, which will be led by a high-profile speaker, bringing together key embassy players to address one or more of the foreign policy issues of the day

- Three free copies of every Foreign Policy Centre publication

- Three free copies of *Global Thinking*, The Foreign Policy Centre's newsletter

- VIP invitations for up to three embassy representatives to all Foreign Policy Centre public events

- Event reports from major Foreign Policy Centre events and seminars

Membership of The Foreign Policy Centre Diplomatic Forum is £500 per year. For further details, please contact Rachel Briggs, rachel@fpc.org.uk

The Foreign Policy Centre Business Partnership

The Foreign Policy Centre also runs a Business Partnership scheme, which aims to bring the business community to the heart of foreign policy thinking.

For more details about this scheme, please contact Rachel Briggs, rachel@fpc.org.uk